SpringerBriefs in Economics

More information about this series at http://www.springer.com/series/8876

Ashima Goyal

History of Monetary Policy in India Since Independence

Springer

Ashima Goyal
Indira Gandhi Institute of Development
Research (IGIDR)
Mumbai
India

ISSN 2191-5504 ISSN 2191-5512 (electronic)
ISBN 978-81-322-1960-6 ISBN 978-81-322-1961-3 (eBook)
DOI 10.1007/978-81-322-1961-3

Library of Congress Control Number: 2014942453

Springer New Delhi Heidelberg New York Dordrecht London

Printed on acid-free paper

Springer is part of Springer Science+Business Media (www.springer.com)

For Niraj

Preface

Actively researching on macroeconomic issues in India's post-reform period, and writing regular op-ed pieces, forced me to develop an analytical framework capable of explaining the outcomes I was writing about. Honing and testing concepts in a real-world laboratory was a great learning experience. Textbook macroeconomic frameworks deal largely with the equilibrium of mature economies, and had to be stretched to apply to a developing economy opening out, deepening markets and undergoing a catch-up process.

Popular pieces in this period were either ideologically motivated, and therefore blind to facts, or driven by short-term market analysis and forecasts. Then history and the fundamental factors affecting the long term were both missing. There was room, therefore, for dispassionate fact-based and fundamentals-based analysis.

So the invitation from Dr. Deshpande to write on India's post-independence monetary history was a wonderful opportunity to systematize this experience and discover more about its roots. The organising framework of a country's structure interacting with the ideas of the time to solidify into institutions that affected outcomes emerged naturally. The first was the slowest moving component. Institutions also are subject to hysteresis and are difficult to alter. But, in the reform period, we saw all this change driven by a new set of ideas. As Rudiger Dornbusch put it, 'In economics, things take longer to happen than you think they will, and then they happen faster than you thought they could'.

In the post-independence period monetary policy, and its specific underlying institutions, changed from being more market-based to government driven and then back to relative market dominance, although of a qualitatively different kind. Both fiscal and market dominance reduce the autonomy of monetary policy. But freer markets and a more open economy are reducing fiscal dominance, and the repeated financial crises moderating the unfettered functioning of markets. As the two are contained, monetary policy can be more effective. Monetary institutions have to evolve towards more autonomy and accountability.

To paraphrase Plato, ideas and institutions are like soil. They either nourish a country and help it grow or they stunt its development, making it wilt and shrink. More openness and freer markets are creating better conditions. But so is their moderation away from extreme free-market positions. An example is the exchange rate. Over this period India experimented with both a fixed exchange rate and a free-market-determined float. Both had adverse outcomes, leading towards managed floating with intervention to prevent excess volatility.

It is rare to have the privilege to watch history in the making and to write about it. I am grateful to: the Professor Brahmananda Endowment Fund for the First Professor P. R. Brahmananda Memorial Research Award to me, for which an earlier version of this manuscript was written, Dr. R. S. Deshpande for his support, two referees for their very encouraging response, Dr. D. M. Nachane and Dr. Y. V. Reddy for useful discussions, and T. C. A. Srinivasa Raghavan for making an unpublished manuscript on pre-independence monetary history available to me.

Over the years, the ideas in this book have been discussed and refined in successive classes I taught, Money and Finance Conferences at IGIDR, the Technical Advisory Committee of the Reserve Bank and in other fora. I thank without implicating Shankar Acharya, Pradeep Agrawal, Pulapre Balakrishnan, N. R. Bhanumurthy, Surjit Bhalla, Saugata Bhattacharya, B. K. Bhoi, Sajjid Chinnoy, Vikas Chitre, Romar Correa, Gangadhar Darbha, Mahendra Dev, Pami Dua, Errol D'Souza, Chetan Ghate, Subir Gokarn, Bimal Jalan, Harun R. Khan, R. Krishnan, Rajiv Kumar, Ashok Lahiri, Rajeev Malick, Sushanta Mallick, Y. H. Malegam, B. M. Misra, Rakesh Mohan, Deepak Mohanty, Sudipto Mundle, P. J. Nayak, Rupa Rege Nitsure, Manoj Panda, B. L. Pandit, V. N. Pandit, Kirit Parikh, Urjit Patel, Michael D. Patra, Raghuram Rajan, Ramkishen Rajan, Indira Rajaraman, Manohar Rao, Subhada Rao, M. Ramachandran, Mridul Saggar, Partha Sen, Parthasarathi Shome, S. L. Shetty, Charan Singh, D. Subbarao, Ganti Subrahmanyam, Rajendra Vaidya, Sonal Varma, Arvind Virmani, Thomas Willett, other colleagues, co-authors and successive batches of students for useful interactions on the topics covered in the book. Shruti Tripathi and Reshma Aguiar provided excellent support in research and in the organisation of material.

I thank the board and management of IGIDR for the creative independence, apart from excellent facilities, which makes the kind of dispassionate assessment attempted in this book possible.

Many publishers were interested in making the award manuscript into a book. I thank them all for their encouragement. Sagarika Ghosh at Springer offered the easier way of a Springer brief. She and Nupoor Singh gave excellent inputs in the publication process.

I thank my family for their indulgence of my esoteric interests. My husband Niraj in particular has acquired expertise by osmosis, is always willing to debate monetary issues and always knows what the interest rate should be! Although being a wonderful grandfather dominates everything else.

Mumbai, May 2014 Ashima Goyal

Contents

About the Author

Ashima Goyal a professor at the Indira Gandhi Institute of Development Research, Mumbai, India, has published widely in institutional and open economy macroeconomics, international finance and governance, and has participated in research projects with ADB, DEA-GOI, GDN, RBI, UN ESCAP and WB. She is the editor of *Handbook on Indian Economy of the 21st century* (OUP India, 2014), co-editor of the journal *Macroeconomics and Finance in Emerging Market Economics* (Routledge), is active in Indian public debate, has served on several boards and policy committees, and is currently a member of the Monetary Policy Technical Advisory Committee. She was also a member of the Working Group on the Operating Procedure of Monetary Policy, 2010. Further, she was a visiting fellow at the Economic Growth Centre, Yale University, USA, and a Fulbright Senior Research Fellow at Claremont Graduate University, USA. Her research has received national and international awards. She won two best research awards at GDN meetings at Tokyo (2000) and Rio de Janeiro (2001); was selected as one of the four most powerful women in economics, a thought leader, by Business Today (2008); and was the first Professor P. R. Brahmananda Memorial Research Grant Awardee.

Abbreviations

AD	Aggregate Demand
AEs	Advanced Economies
AS	Aggregate Supply
BIS	Bank of International Settlements
CAD	Current Account Deficit
CBLO	Collateralized Borrowing and Lending Obligation
CBs	Central Banks
CCIL	Clearing Corporation of India
CMR	Call Money Rate
CPI	Consumer Price Index
CRR	Cash Reserve Ratio
CSSs	Central Sponsored Schemes
DSGE	Dynamic Stochastic General Equilibrium
EMs	Emerging Markets
FD	Fiscal Deficit
FDI	Foreign Direct Investment
FIIs	Foreign Institution Investors
FPI	Foreign Portfolio Investment
FPLL	Fuel, Power, Light and Lubricants
FRBM	Fiscal Responsibility and Budget Management
FSB	Financial Stability Board
FX	Foreign Exchange
G	Government Expenditure
G-20	The Group of Twenty
GDCF	Gross Domestic Capital Formation
GDP	Gross Domestic Product
GDS	Gross Domestic Saving
GFA	Global Financial Architecture
GFC	Global Financial Crisis
GMM	Generalized Method of Moments
Gsecs	Government Securities

IMF	International Monetary Fund
LAF	Liquidity Adjustment Facility
LAS	Longer Run Aggregate Supply
M3	Broad Money
MGNREGS	Mahatma Gandhi National Rural Employment Guarantee Scheme
MIBOR	Mumbai Interbank Offered Rate
MSF	Marginal Standing Facility
NDA	Net Domestic Assets
NDF	Non-deliverable Forward
NFA	Net Foreign Assets
NX	Net Exports
OMOs	Open Market Operations
OTC	Over-the-Counter
PC	Phillips Curve
PFCE	Private Final Consumption Expenditure
QE	Quantitative Easing
RBI	Reserve Bank of India
RD	Revenue Deficit
RM	Reserve Money
SCP	Structure, Conduct, Performance
SIIO	Structure-Ideas-Institutions-Outcomes Paradigm
SLR	Statutory Liquidity Ratio
T-bills	Treasury Bills
UIP	Uncovered Interest Parity
VAR	Vector Autoregression
WB	World Bank
WMA	Ways and Means Advance
WPI	Wholesale Price Index

Chapter 1
Structure, Ideas, and Institutions

Abstract In developing a SIIO paradigm, based on structure and ideas that become engraved in institutions and affect outcomes, to examine and assess monetary policy in India after independence, this chapter surveys relevant aspects of Indian structure, the ideas that influenced monetary policy formation and evolution, and the institutional framework, procedures, and norms of practice in which policy was carried out. Even in a broad brush focus on the main trends, a flavor is given of intricate processes that generate the cold numbers.

Keywords Country structure · Monetary theories · Institutions · Policy norms · Processes

1.1 Introduction

This book examines and assesses monetary policy in India after independence in the context of interplay between domestic structure and external factors. Domestic structure includes economic and political structure, the demands of growth, poverty reduction, financial inclusion, and the gradual development of institutions and markets. The external sector includes the dominant ideas of the time and their change, shocks such as oil and wars, dependence on foreign capital, and the effect of greater opening out. Structure and ideas become engraved in institutions that affect outcomes. Instead of the structure, conduct, and performance (SCP) paradigm used in the industrial organization literature, this is a SIIO paradigm.[1]

[1] Since the book is a revised version of a monograph written for the first Professor Brahmananda Memorial Research Award, its approach is very much in the tradition set by Dr. Brahmananda. He had himself undertaken a monumental study of money, income, and prices in nineteenth-century India (2001). But starting with his early work (Vakil and Brahmananda 1956), a defining characteristic of his approach was to refine analytical frameworks so that they became relevant for the analysis of Indian structure. Nachane (2003) brings out, with great warmth and affection, both Dr. Brahmananda's scholarship and his focus on relevance.

A. Goyal, *History of Monetary Policy in India Since Independence*,
SpringerBriefs in Economics, DOI 10.1007/978-81-322-1961-3_1

In this book, narrative history, data analysis, and reporting of research are used to show the dialectic between ideas and structure. Policy outcomes are explained in the framework developed. Given the six decades over which the dialectic has played out, a broad brush approach is used that focuses on the main trends, rather than the day-to-day policy decisions that co-created the trends. But a flavor is given of intricate processes that generate the cold numbers. Time series charts as well as decadal annual rates of growth and ratios are reported for many macroeconomic variables. Data for a few post-global financial crisis (GFC) years are also analyzed since this was a source of rich macroeconomic variations.

It is argued a greater congruence between ideas and structure in recent times contributed to improvements in institutions and to India's better performance notwithstanding some problems due to fallout from the GFC. Policy moved from struggling with scarcity to having to deal with excess foreign capital inflows. Automatic financing of government deficits gave way to more independence for the Reserve Bank, but political pressures led to a uniquely Indian balancing between reducing inflation yet promoting growth.

The distinctive feature of this book is it is not an official history like those currently available, but an independent academic work that is closer to the international and to Indian academic literature, while it draws on the Indian experience largely from published materials, including official records. There is a brief introduction to structural aspects that impinge upon monetary policy in India in Sect. 1.2. Section 1.3 follows the development of international and national ideas about the working of monetary policy; Sect. 1.4 shows how institutions that were set up, procedures, and norms of practice that were established affected monetary policy in India. The analytical framework of this chapter helps to understand actual policy actions and their outcomes analyzed in Chap. 2.

1.2 Structure

The most important aspect of India's structure is the high population density and the high proportion of the population in less productive occupations. The Hindu rate of growth (as Raj Krishna christened it) of below five percent per annum, for much of the period, meant that even in 2012, average per capita income was only about 1489.2 USD per capita and more than 50 % of the population remained in rural areas.

1.2.1 Sectors

Steady development did bring down the share of agriculture and allied activities in total income from 52 % in 1950–1951 to 30 prereform and 13.7 in 2013, but since the population dependent on agriculture had not fallen commensurately, inequality

Table 1.1 Sectoral contribution to growth (share of major sectors in GDP at factor cost) (base year 2004–2005)

At constant prices	Agriculture	Industry	Services
1950–1951 to 1959–1960	41.23	12.23	35.12
1960–1961 to 1969–1970	35.06	15.62	39.91
1970–1971 to 1979–1980	31.44	17.3	42.78
1980–1981 to 1989–1990	27.74	19.33	46.92
1990–1991 to 1999–2000	22.54	20.8	52.31
2000–2001 to 2009–2010	15.77	20.36	60.94
2010–2011 to 2012–2013	11.99	19.63	66.29

increased. Poverty ratios had fallen with growth, and literacy had increased, but given the one billion plus population, absolute numbers below the poverty line also remained at above 300 million and illiteracy above 30 %. The proportion of population in the most productive age group of 20–59 reached about 50 % by 2010. This implied a large expansion in the work force needing to be equipped with the appropriate skills.[2]

Table 1.1 gives the decadal averages, showing the changes in sectoral composition. Over the years, the economy changed from being agriculture dominant to services dominant. The share of industry increased, but remained low at about 20 %. Post-reform higher growth was driven by various service sectors, industry also grew after 2000, but basic utilities such as electricity and water, which had done better in the previous 2 decades, slowed (Table 1.2). Their post-reform period growth was much below historical values. Services grew much faster, while construction regained its 1960s peak growth. By the end of the period, agriculture had again touched its best 1980s rate of growth of 4 %.

1.2.2 Growth and Inflation

Financial markets were quite active at the time of independence; interest rates were market determined; an incipient bill market was also developed. But according to the ideas of the time, planning was extended to cover the monetary and financial system also. To support planned development, with the commanding heights for capital-intensive public sector projects, the emphasis was on generating resources for public investment, allocating resources to priority sectors, and expanding the reach of the formal financial system.

After a good initial start with the first and second five-year plans, the system was unable to raise growth rates or moderate the supply-side shocks the economy was subject to.

[2] The original source for the data processed in tables and charts, unless otherwise mentioned, are the Web sites of the Reserve Bank of India (RBI) and the CSO.

Table 1.2 Growth of real GDP in major sectors (base year 2004–2005)

At constant prices (2004–2005)	GDP at factor cost	Agriculture and allied activities	Agriculture	Industry	Mining and quarrying	Manufacturing	Electricity, gas, and water supply	Services	Construction	Trade, hotels, transport, and communication	Financing, insurance, real estate, and business services	Community, social, and personal services
Average annual growth rate												
1950–1951 to 1959–1960	3.59	2.72	2.98	5.76	4.65	5.87	10.7	4.2	5.76	5.02	3.07	3.51
1960–1961 to 1969–1970	3.96	2.51	2.52	6.18	6.19	5.89	11.43	5.19	7.18	5.34	3.21	5.24
1970–1971 to 1979–1980	2.94	1.26	1.41	4.29	3.05	4.31	6.91	3.94	1.95	4.71	4.31	4.13
1980–1981 to 1989–1990	5.58	4.41	4.67	6.41	8.71	5.77	8.5	6.34	4.83	5.96	8.67	6
1990–1991 to 1999–2000	5.8	3.24	3.29	5.8	4.87	5.84	7.26	7.24	5.63	7.77	8.02	6.68
2000–2001 to 2009–2010	7.25	2.46	2.48	7.31	4.37	8.05	5.68	8.78	9.31	9.68	9.42	6.39
2010–2011 to 2012–2013	6.84	4.5	4.81	4.2	1.24	4.49	5.28	8.16	6.71	8.58	10.12	5.62

Table 1.3 Average annual inflation

	WPI (all commodities)	WPI (primary goods)	WPI (of which food articles)	WPI (of which non-food articles)	WPI (FPLL)	WPI (manufacturing)	CPI (IW)
1953–1954 to 1959–1960	2.48	-	2.94	-	2.30	1.62	-
196019–61 to 1969–1970	6.34	-	7.43	-	5.03	4.92	-
1970–1971 to 1979–1980	8.97	8.95	7.24	8.56	12.15	9.03	9.32
1980–1981 to 1989–1990	7.98	7.76	8.57	7.70	9.21	7.86	8.48
1990–1991 to 1999–2000	8.12	9.37	10.24	8.31	10.57	7.13	8.73
2000–2001 to 2009–2010	5.28	5.68	5.27	5.65	8.05	4.34	6.75
2010–2011 to 2012–2013	8.62	12.45	10.93	14.17	12.19[a]	6.12	11.72

Note Base 1982 for the years 1953–1954 to 2009–2010; base 2004–2005 for the years 2010–2011 to 2012–2013
[a]figures for fuel and power only

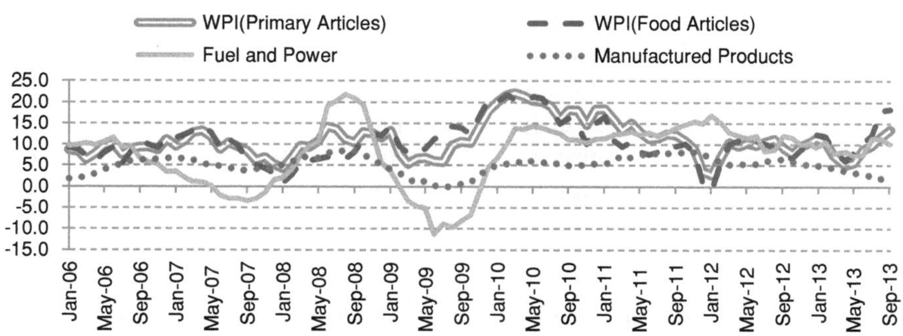

Chart 1.1 Year-on-year inflation rate 2006–2013

Table 1.3 shows that decadal average inflation rates were dominated by primary goods and fuel, power, light, and lubricants (FPLL) inflation. Liberalization, soft global prices, and the effect of competition from abroad reduced primary good and manufacturing inflation in 2000s, but the severe international food and oil price shocks pushed it up again from 2007 (Chart 1.1).

Ambitious projects in the second five-year plan, and a paucity of resources, made the government soon turn to deficit financing funded by ad hoc treasury bills (T bills) (Chart 1.2). In these years, the Reserve Bank of India (RBI) lost its initial independence (see Section IV), and its primary responsibility became to find

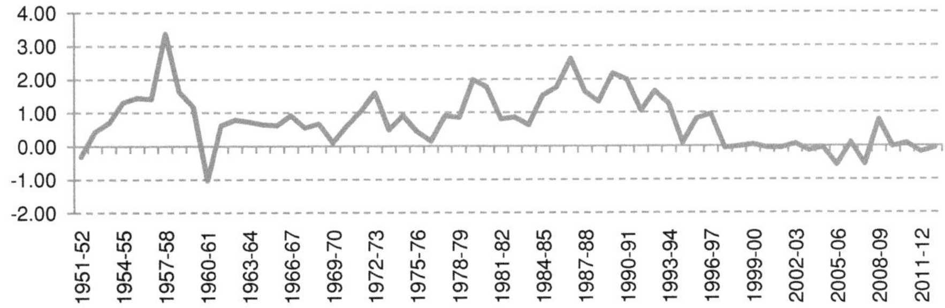

Chart 1.2 Budgetary deficit of the central government (as a % to GDP)

Table 1.4 Savings, investment, and consumption (Rs billion) (base year 2004–2005)

	GDCF	PFCE	GDS
Average annual growth rate			
1950–1951 to 1959–1960	10.65	5.36	7.89
1960–1961 to 1969–1970	12.81	9.61	13.55
1970–1971 to 1979–1980	15.25	10.46	15.31
1980–1981 to 1989–1990	16.70	13.70	15.71
1990–1991 to 1999–2000	16.75	14.25	17.28
2000–2001 to 2009–2010	16.51	10.99	15.91
2010–2011 to 2012–2013	14.30	15.93	11.87
(*As a percentage of GDP at current market price* (GDPmp))			
1950–1951 to 1959–1960	11.68	94.72	10.51
1960–1961 to 1969–1970	15.08	87.52	13.08
1970–1971 to 1979–1980	17.99	81.68	17.85
1980–1981 to 1989–1990	20.96	76.69	19.13
1990–1991 to 1999–2000	25.05	67.87	23.66
2000–2001 to 2009–2010	31.24	60.35	30.66
2010–2011 to 2011–2013	35.62	56.72	31.71

resources for government expenditure. It always had a commitment to developmental functions such as expanding credit to agriculture and other priority sectors. In addition, in a democracy with a large number of poor, high inflation was not acceptable. Therefore, tight control was kept on aggregate credit and money supply, while selective credit controls were used to direct credit in line with plan priorities (see Section V).

The push toward inclusive financial deepening, especially the expansion of bank branches after nationalization, probably contributed to the sharp rise in the gross domestic savings (GDS) to GDP ratio in the 1970s. Another large jump came in the post-reform high growth period, and the growth rate of GDS overtook that of gross domestic capital formation (GDCF) and private final consumption expenditure (PFCE) (Table 1.4). But this reversed after the GFC as savings slowed more than GDCF, thus increasing dependence on foreign savings. Growth rates fell more than GDCF since governance bottlenecks delayed projects, raising the capital–output ratio.

India has a healthy combination of savings to finance investment and consumption to create demand. But the savings are poorly intermediated through the financial sector, and even in 2013, less than half of the population had a bank account. This also raised dependence on foreign savings, especially for firms, since government appropriated a large share of bank lending.

1.2.3 Politics

A majoritarian democratic regime, such as India, has a bias toward targeted transfers at the expense of public goods, compared to a regime based on proportional voting. Political fragmentation, after the first 20 years of independence when the Congress party provided a stable government, made matters worse. As the Congress lost dominance and intense multiparty competition set in, populist schemes multiplied. With multiple competing parties, swing votes become critical for winning in a first-past-the-post system. In such an environment, after the oil shocks of the 1970s, several user charges for public goods were kept fixed, although costs were rising. Subsidies, transfers, and distortions increased, while current and future provision of public goods suffered. Table 1.2 shows the sharp fall in growth rates for essential public goods such as water and electricity from the 1970s.

By the 1980s, populist Central-Sponsored Schemes (CSSs) became a way for the central government to directly reach the masses, sidestepping the constitutionally mandated Finance Commissions, that were meant to ensure a uniform level of public services in the Federal structure. The setting up of the Planning Commission to oversee the top-down planning process had already weakened non-discretionary devolution to the States (Goyal 2014).

New CSSs were announced every year, although targeting was poor and waste and corruption proliferated. Since state elections were separated from those at the Center in 1971, frequent elections kept populist pressure up continually and harmed long-term development. The first reaction of new caste-based parties to the acquisition of power was consumption transfers to their support groups, especially as a belief in a vibrant future was missing since the development policies of the past had not delivered growth. Once in power, they were concerned with "loot" in order to buy votes and legislators in the future. Institutions of governance were undermined. In the south where the caste-based movement was older, progressive reform, emphasizing education and capacity building, was achieved (Goyal 2003).

The objective of providing government services at affordable prices led to cross-subsidization both in the provision of specific products and across government functions. Low price caps for many public goods led to systematic incentives to lower quality and investment. Thus, falling efficiency and rising costs compounded the problem of low user charges and prevented a natural fall in prices from improvements in technology and organization. But where the government had monopoly power and was servicing the rich, prices were raised much above costs of production. Or indirect charges, not obvious to voters, such as the prices of intermediate goods, were raised. As the rich turned to private providers, revenue losses contributed to the inability to service the poor adequately. The cross-subsidization was not sufficient to cover costs. The choices made amounted to protecting the poor through current transfers, rather than building their assets and human capital, when it was the latter that was the sustainable option. This was a rational social outcome because the rich could often escape imposts in the long term, and the poor had high discount rates and pessimistic growth projections, so they were willing to forego future growth for current subsidies.

1.2.4 Government Finances

As these effects cumulated, the revenue deficit became positive. That is, government consumption exceeded its income. Chart 1.3 shows that the first year the revenue deficit (RD) became positive was 1980–1981, and after that, government consumption always exceeded its income or revenue. RD is the amount the government needs to borrow to finance its own consumption. The government's borrowing in any year to finance current and capital expenditure net of tax and non-tax revenue is its fiscal deficit. The primary deficit is the fiscal deficit minus interest payments. Since this is net of the burden of servicing debts due to past borrowing, it is a measure of current borrowing and of fresh addition to government debt. This, along with interest payments, adds to government debt. Chart 1.3 shows that the fiscal and primary deficits that had risen earlier to finance public investment began to fall after the reforms. The primary deficit even became briefly negative, but given the burden of interest payments on past debt, the RD could not fall until interest rates fell and tax buoyancy was established in 2003. All three deficits shot up again with the fiscal stimulus after the GFC, and fiscal compression was slow. But the much larger share of the RD showed the shift in the composition of government expenditure from investment to subsidies.

In the early years, the only deficit concept used was that of budget deficit (Chart 1.2). This was the change in outstanding T bills, government deposits, and

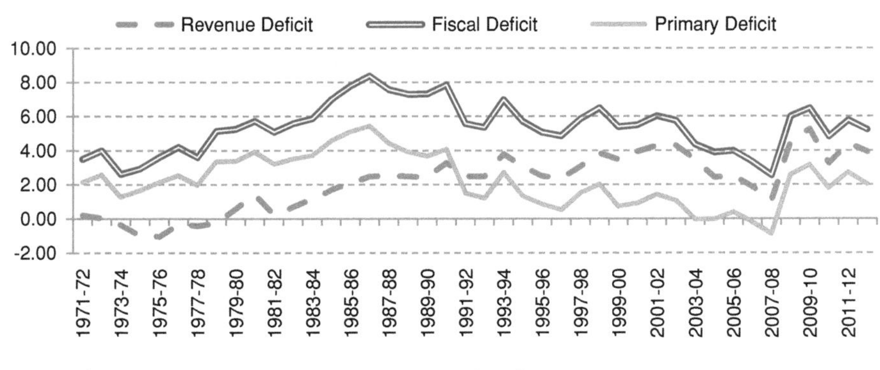

Chart 1.3 Deficit of the central government (as a % to GDP)

Table 1.5 Center's fiscal position

Average annual growth rates	Revenue receipt	Tax revenue	Non-tax revenue	Total expenditure	Revenue expenditure	Capital expenditure
1950–1951 to 1959–1960	-	-	-	14.65	9.08	25.80
1960–1961 to 1969–1970	-	-	-	13.55	15.23	12.34
1970–1971 to 1979–1980	15.44	15.23	13.65	14.37	17.00	11.57
1980–1981 to 1989–1990	16.42	16.24	19.32	17.31	18.57	15.05
1990–1991 to 1999–2000	13.86	13.15	15.01	12.44	14.54	6.37
2000–2001 to 2009–2010	9.79	14.03	8.55	13.33	14.08	13.33
2010–2011 to 2012–2013	16.32	17.63	16.76	11.84	11.49	15.34
(As a percentage of GDPmp)						
1950–1951 to 1959–1960	-	-	-	6.85	3.70	3.15
1960–1961 to 1969–1970	-	-	-	12.05	5.65	6.39
1970–1971 to 1979–1980	10.67	6.59	2.01	14.30	8.26	6.04
1980–1981 to 1989–1990	12.56	7.29	2.36	17.56	11.38	6.18
1990–1991 to 1999–2000	12.23	6.77	2.46	16.00	12.25	3.75
2000–2001 to 2009–2010	9.41	7.10	2.31	15.18	12.76	2.42
2010–2011 to 2012–2013	11.14	7.11	2.34	16.16	12.46	3.70

other cash balances with the RBI. The budget deficit underestimated the monetary impact of the deficit since it did not include RBI holdings of dated Government securities (Gsecs). The RBI largely held the treasury bills. To the extent they were held by banks, their monetary impact was reduced. RBI credit to the government gives the correct monetary impact of fiscal operations. After 1996, when automatic monetization of the deficit was reduced, and government funding by banks increased, the budget deficit fell (Chart 1.2).

As fund constraints appeared, it was easiest for the government to reduce investment, while maintaining populist schemes. This strategy continued in the post-reform period. Table 1.5 shows the trend rise in revenue expenditure and the sharp fall in capital expenditure. It does not include States' revenue and expenditure, since only the Center's finances have implications for monetary policy. States' borrowing is restricted.

Table 1.6 Deficit of central government

(As a percentage of GDPmp)	Revenue deficit	Fiscal deficit	Primary deficit
1970–1971 to 1979–1980	−0.29	3.86	2.33
1980–1981 to 1989–90	1.72	6.75	4.14
1990–1991 to 1999–2000	3.02	5.89	1.65
2000–2001 to 2009–2010	3.35	4.77	0.84
2010–2011 to 2012–2013	3.84	5.25	2.18

The cuts in public investment allowed some improvement in the fiscal and primary deficit that was specially marked after 2000 (Table 1.6), a period of tax buoyancy due to reform and higher growth. Fiscal responsibility legislation also contributed, but was overturned by the global crisis. The revenue deficit,[3] however, remained high as committed populist expenditures were difficult to cut. There was an argument that some expenditures essential to build human capacity were classified as current when they were actually capital expenditure since they improve the stock of human capital. But expenditures once implemented set in self-sustaining dynamics partly by creating interest groups or constituencies they favor. In more recent periods, moreover, delivery and governance have begun to matter for electoral performance as they are necessary to utilize the opportunities growth creates, even for the less well-off.

The government accumulated debt since it was borrowing for consumption, earning very low returns on its investments, and its expenditures were not successful for a long time in improving growth and taxes. High growth improved many parameters in the 2000s, but the fall in growth after the euro debt crisis reduced revenue growth, although higher inflation did reduce debt.

Even as monetary policy got some degrees of freedom from fiscal dominance due to legislative restraints, fluctuations in capital flows after reforms created new constraints. After this brief review of the structure within which monetary policy had to operate, we turn to the ideas that influenced policy.

1.3 Ideas

India may have become a closed economy for much of the period, but it has always been quite open to global academic ideas. The dialectic between these and structure, needs, and the domestic political and economic debate affected policies adopted.

1.3.1 Keynes Modified

The 1950s was the period when Keynesian ideas dominated. Particularly following theGreat Depression, government expenditure was thought to be the dominant macroeconomic tool. But the Indian debate was more nuanced. VKRV Rao (1952)

[3] The table starts from 1970 to 1971 since before that only the budget deficit was reported.

argued that pervasive supply bottlenecks could be expected to make demand stimuli ineffective in a country like India. It was government investment that was to take the lead in relieving supply bottlenecks through the plan expenditures. Financing these expenditures was an obvious concern. Indian policy followed Keynesian ideas in giving government expenditure pride of place, with monetary policy to support it. But the expenditure was to expand supply rather than to create demand. Policy was also Keynesian in giving priority to quantity adjustment and intervention over price. Monetarists tended to favor the use of markets with the role of the government restricted to creating an enabling environment for the private sector; Keynesians were more interventionist—favoring discretionary monetary and fiscal policies.

RBI was committed to the development of the nation, from the beginning. In the context of large planned expenditure, it was natural to emphasize credit and its allocation to productive uses. But ensuring credit availability for the government and priority sectors, while meeting aggregate targets, meant restricting credit to other sectors. In the beginning, interest rates were market determined, but market-led allocation was discouraged in favor of policy-led rationing of quantities. The influential UK Radcliffe committee (1958) provided support for these policies. Among its recommendations were that government debt and market liquidity management should be the focus of monetary policy, and too large interest rate variations disturb markets.

A variety of devices were used to intervene in credit allocation. Apart from general credit guidelines to direct bank credit to priority sectors, selective credit controls were used, for example, to limit advances against certain commodities to mitigate speculative hoarding. But at the same time, banks were forced to finance the large credit needs of the government food procurement and distribution system.

Following the USSR model and the ideas of Mahalanobis, the plans favored a big push to develop indigenous heavy industry. Vakil and Brahmananda (1956) pointed out early that in an economy like India, the critical constraint was likely to be wage goods, requiring focus on agriculture. They noted that in a developed country, the rate of growth of capital equals that of population and gives its rate of growth, whereas in an underdeveloped country, the potential workforce exceeds capital stock. Development that raises per capita incomes must involve a period where the rate of growth exceeds that of population; the constraint that prevents this, and sustains underemployment, is the supply of wage goods. Structural rigidities did influence early thinking at the RBI (Pendharkar and Narasimham 1966), but it led to quantitative credit allocation over the use of general interest rate instruments in order to encourage development activity and lower the cost of government borrowing . A satisfactory combination of key monetary and structural features has proved elusive in both Indian Keynesian-Structuralist and Monetarist models.[4]

The inward-looking import-substituting approach led to a severe foreign exchange constraint. The foreign exchange regulation act 1974 was used to

[4] Krishnamurthy and Pandit (1985), Rakshit (2009), and Balakrishna (1994) are fine examples of structuralist thinking in the Indian context. Jadhav (1990) surveys monetary models.

implement strict rationing of foreign exchange, with heavy regulation of markets. Neglect of the wage goods constraint in planning exercises meant inflation soon surfaced. But the response to this was monetary. The acceptance of the economy as supply and not demand constrained, together with the political sensitivity to inflation, meant that restriction on aggregate money supply growth was regarded as the answer to inflation. It was also regarded as the answer to widening government deficits. Increasing the statutory liquidity and compulsory reserve ratios of commercial banks both financed government spending and restricted aggregate money supply growth even as reserve bank credit to the government continued to increase.

1.3.2 Monetarism in the Aggregate

In Keynes view, money was regarded as having limited impact on the real sector because of low interest elasticities and a possible liquidity trap. Indian interest elasticity of demand was low in the early years, and the quantity theory of money linking the money supply to the price level was largely accepted as the analytical framework underpinning the supply of money.[5] Given reasonable predictability of money demand and the money multiplier, monetary targeting was feasible if reserve money could be controlled. Rising income elasticity of money demand could be factored in. Given automatic financing of the budget deficit, raising the reserve ratios was a way to control reserve money.

Estimations largely gave a stable money demand,[6] when enhanced to include variables relevant in the Indian context, such as relative shares of agriculture and non-agricultural output and the degree of monetization.[7] Interest elasticity was low,[8] and income elasticity of demand for broad money was about 1.5–2 (Gupta 1976; Vasudevan 1977). On the supply side, the money multiplier (that multiplied the reserve money to generate the money stock) was also stable. So it was thought

---

[5] In Irving Fisher's version, the quantity theory of money is written as $MV = PY$. With constant velocity (V) and output (Y) at full employment, there is a one-to-one relation of money supply (M) and the price level (P). Velocity would change with the factors affecting the demand for money such as income and the nominal interest rate. But predictable or stable changes in money demand could be factored into arrive at money supply targets.

[6] As late as 1995, Rao and Singh argued that in spite of the overwhelming international evidence on instability of money demand, Indian money, income and a relevant interest rate were cointegrated, demonstrating long-run stability. Even so, their view was that targeting of nominal income, or velocity, is superior to targeting some monetary aggregate, since velocity can be derived independently or residually, without trying to invert a questionable money demand schedule.

[7] Brahmananda's (2001) monetary history was based on the quantity theory of money following Friedman and Schwartz's (1971) famous US history, but he modified it to suit nineteenth-century India, for example, by including an index of rainfall as a determinant of the price level and an index of monetization as a determinant of velocity.

[8] This was not surprising, given that markets were suppressed. Preindependence studies had found significant interest elasticities (Anjaneyulu et al. 2010).

possible to obtain the required rate of growth of money supply by adjusting the growth of reserve money by changes in the reserve ratio. For money supply to be used to determine prices, the first step is for the RBI to be able to control money supply.

The money multiplier shows how broad money (M) can be created as a multiple of base or high-powered money (H) given the currency deposit (C/D) and bank reserves to deposit ratio (R/D). The multiplier decreases with both C/D and R/D, since both decrease the credit banks can generate from a given base.[9] In the 1970s, the RBI followed a balance sheet approach for determining the components of money supply. This assumed the money multiplier to be constant even in incremental terms. But C/D can be expected to fall, for example, as bank branches rise. An adjusted multiplier corrects for changes in cash reserves.

A number of authors sought to obtain more accurate predictions of the money multiplier and improve the analytical understanding of money supply determination (Gupta1976; Singh et al. 1982; Rangarajan and Singh 1984). Forecasting exercises included Rao et al. (1981), Chitre (1986), and Nachane and Ray (1989). The studies were an important policy input. To target the money stock from a given base or high-powered money, it was necessary to predict the money multiplier, so that bank's contribution to raising money supply could be quantified.

But macroeconomic variables are determined in a complex inter active process. The studies did not adequately analyze the interactions between the players who determine money supply. They ignored feedback, simultaneous equation bias, and identification problems. Even in 1959, banks found legitimate ways to expand credit demand to meet rising despite higher reserve requirements. They reduced cash in hand and excess balances with the RBI, sold Gsecs (dated government securities), and maintained large outstandings on RBI accommodation, thus liquidating investments rather than reducing advances as they were expected to. The RBI's response was to make access to its financing temporary to try and close loopholes (Balachandran 1998 pp. 79–80).

If banks managed some autonomy to maximize profits even in a regime of direct credit controls, then these strategies can be expected to dominate in a liberalized era. Money demand will become unstable as close financial substitutes develop. Although loans create deposits, loans are determined both by supply and by demand. They depend on profit maximization by banks and on RBI monetary policy that changes base money.

Dash and Goyal (2000) found money supply to be neither fully endogenous nor fully controlled in a new specification employed to test for the degree of endogeneity of commercial bank credit and its response to structural variables relevant to the Indian context. They used the variable M-H to identify money supply in a single equation and disentangle the contribution of the central and the commercial banks

[9] M = mH, where m is derived from the two identities M = C + D and H = C + R by dividing the first from the second and then dividing the numerator and denominator by $1/D$ to get M = ((1 + C/D)/(R/D + C/D)) H (Goodhart 2007). The multiplier can also be written as m = [(D/R)(1 + D/C)/(D/R + D/C)] by multiplying the right side by [(D/CR)/(D/CR)]. The multiplier reduces when (D/R) or (D/C) falls.

to the money supply process over 1960–1961 to 1992–1993. They found that bank credit reacted more to financial variables and had dissimilar responses to food and manufacturing prices and output. Credit turned out to be the endogenous outcome of incentives facing agents. But in the data set, as interest rates were imperfectly flexible, a range of price variables carried these incentives. Whenever incentives to expand credit were high enough, banks found ways around a variety of quantitative controls. They suggested that price bubbles in assets that lead to expansions in broad money could be better controlled through tax-based regulation.

Although the RBI could affect base money, banks were able to circumvent controls and expand credit when there were profits to be made. Money supply had been somewhat exogenous, but fundamental changes were occurring that made it more endogenous.

1.3.3 Globalization: Ideas and Domestic Impact

In the 1970s, the developed world had moved to the float as the dollar was delinked from gold and had gradually begun to open capital accounts. Liberalization and deepening financial markets made monetary policy more effective, faster, and less subject to political delays compared to fiscal policy. Its use, therefore, dominated macrostabilization from the 1980s.

Ricardian equivalence-type arguments suggested that private actions would counter fiscal policy. For example, if government spent more, taxpayers foreseeing a rise in future taxes would save more. This would reduce the effect of government spending on demand. Long lags and political constraints on fiscal policy were also being recognized as weakening fiscal policy (Blanchard et al. 2010). Markets were dominating governments, and price adjustments were dominating quantity adjustments, once again. The instruments Central Banks (CBs) were using worldwide were interest rates. The classical neutrality of money doctrine held that real interest rates were determined by productivity and invariant to policy. Sargeant showed that an interest rate instrument could make the system unstable. But these results held only if money was the only nominal standard. Sticky wages and prices create an alternative that fixes nominal variables and allow real interest rates to be influenced by policy for considerable periods. Moreover, an interest rate rule that responded to macroeconomic variables such as output and inflation gaps could be stable (Goodhart 2007).

As globalization and financial innovations occur, interest rates can be expected to affect domestic expenditures significantly. Deeper financial markets spread the effects more widely. Interest rates play a larger role in the transmission of monetary policy and become the natural instrument of monetary policy, although other channels of transmission, such as credit, continue to be important. First, interest rates become more flexible and responsive to CB intervention; second, the interest rate becomes a more sensitive and fast signal of potential imbalances; third, demand for broad money becomes unstable and enhancement in its supply from commercial banks more flexible, so that targeting monetary aggregates becomes difficult, and the attempt causes high volatility in interest rates; and fourth, the size of foreign exchange, bond, equity, and other asset markets rises. These markets are very sensitive to interest rates. Now, forward-looking behaviorbecomes more important, and markets try to guess the CB's response to uncertainty and to shocks. Thus, transparency becomes a major issue. As markets develop, the reason that most CBs start targeting interest rates is that it becomes necessary for market stability. A fractional banking system and leveraged financial sector must have funds available whenever required in order to function. It is necessary for the operation of interbank markets.

In India, however, the entire interest rate structure was still administered, financial–real sector links were weak, markets underdeveloped as quantity rationing was in force, so estimated interest elasticities of aggregate aggregate and money demand were low. The dualistic structure and limited reach of the modern financial sector implied low interest elasticities (Rakshit 2009). But the deleterious effects of quantitative controls were beginning to be recognized. The perception that India was stuck at a low 1 % per capita growth, while countries that had opened out in the 1960s, such as South Korea, were doing much better, was becoming common. The Chakravarty Committee (RBI 1985) set up to review the working of the monetary system wrote:

> …there does appear to be a strong case for greater reliance on the interest rate instrument with a view to promoting the effective use of credit, and in short-term monetary management. Over the years quantitative controls on credit have increasingly borne the major burden of adjustment required under anti-inflationary policies and have in the process given rise to distortions in credit allocations at the micro level (pp. 161–162).

Although it opted for an overall monetary targeting approach, the committee did warn that in an economy like India with structural rigidities, supply shocks, and structural changes, a monetary growth rate must not be mechanically implemented, but should be seen rather as an indicative, flexible, target range. It suggested a range around 14 % for broad money growth, based on an averageoutput growth of 5 %, inflation at 4 %, and income elasticity of broad money demand of 2.

It suggested a greater role for the interest rate in influencing the demand for credit, thus reducing the sole reliance on rationing the supply of credit and allowing more productive credit allocation.[10] It advocated more market holding of treasury bills (for short-term finance) and Gsecs. A retail market for Gsecs was also to be encouraged. These alternative avenues for government borrowing were expected to give the RBI greater freedom to use open market operations (OMOs), or sale and purchase of Gsecs both outright and repos, to control reserve money. As interest rates rose, a fall in capital value would militate against higher voluntary holdings, so it was suggested that the valuation of Gsecs held to satisfy SLR be based on purchase price and not on market value.

Narasimham Committee (RBI 1991) echoed these concerns, as did the working group on the money market (RBI 1987).

> "The committee is of the view that the SLR instrument should be deployed in conformity with the original intention of regarding it as a prudential requirement and not be viewed as

[10] Even banks used a system of cash credit rather than bills and loans to finance working capital, which reduced their supervision of the end use of credit.

> a major instrument for financing the public sector (RBI 1991, p. iv)" and the next recommendation on p. v "..proposes that the Reserve Bank consider progressively reducing the cash reserve ratio from its present high level. With the deregulation of interest rates there would be more scope for the use of open market operations by the Reserve Bank with correspondingly less emphasis on variations in the cash reserve ratio."

Low returns from deficit financed public investment and growth stagnation in a protected economy contributed to worsening deficits and accumulating debt. This faltering of fiscal policy in India was bolstered by international changes in dominant ideas.

While the original Keynesian position had been that fiscal policy was generally more effective than monetary policy, the New Keynesian view was that interest rates were effective in closing the output gap, given wage–price rigidities, except in extreme liquidity traps. Even the original Monetarist position was misunderstood. Friedman's famous quote about money being a veil and having no effect on the real sector has an important rider:

> Money is a veil. The "real" forces are the capabilities of the people, their industry and ingenuity, the resources they command, their mode of economic and political organization, and the like (Friedman and Schwartz 1971, p. 606).... Perfectly true. Yet also somewhat misleading, unless we recognize that there is hardly a contrivance man possesses which can do more damage to society when it goes amiss (p. 607). This was to be expected from a monetary history that covered the Great Depression.

They also identified the fundamental reasons that create problems from both too tight and too loose monetary policies. Too tight policies can destroy the financial system since:

> Each bank thinks it can determine how much of its assets it can hold in the form of currency, plus deposits at the Federal Reserve Banks, to meet legal reserve requirements and for precautionary purposes. Yet the total amount available for all banks to hold is outside the control of all banks together (p. 607).

But too loose can destroy confidence in the currency:

> ...that common and widely accepted medium of exchange is, at bottom, a social convention which owes its very existence to the mutual acceptance of what from one point of view is a fiction.

The monetary squeeze was particularly tight in India after the oil shocks of the 1970s and had a high output cost. But a better synthesis of Keynesian and Monetarist ideas was becoming feasible.

1.3.4 New Keynesian Theories in Emerging Markets

The New Keynesian Economics (NKE) school (Clarida et al. 1999, 2001; Woodford 2003) demonstrates how monetary policy can work effectively through an interest rate instrument that reacts to expected inflation. Results are based on simple IS (investment equals savings) and Phillips curves (PC) that are derived from rigorous optimization by agents with Foresight. They differ, therefore, from standard formulations in the strong theoretical foundations, which make them robust to policy shocks[11] and give them forward-looking behavior.

The IS curve relates the output gap, or excess demand, inversely to the real interest rate, positively to expected future demand and to a positive demand shock. The PC curve relates inflation positively to the output gap, to future expected inflation, and to a cost-push or supply shock. The output gap is defined as the gap between actual output and potential output. The PC relates inflation to the output gap rather than unemployment and to cost-push. This, and the explicit modeling of relevant rigidities and distortions, makes it relevant to Indian conditions. Even though it is difficult to measure unemployment, an output gap can be defined for India. The idea of potential output and expected future changes in it are useful for an economy undertaking structural reform. Second, cost-push factors play a dominant role in inflation (Goyal 2002).

Such a PC is derived assuming a certain probability that administered and other prices will remain fixed in any period. When a price is varied, it is set as a function of the expected future marginal cost. A proportionate relationship is assumed between the output gap and marginal cost. A cost shock, then, is anything that disturbs this relationship. Such deviations can occur due to administered prices, wage expectations markup, exchange rate shocks, infrastructure bottlenecks, and rising transaction costs in an emerging market. Some of these shocks affect averageas well as marginal costssince they do not only affect activity at the margin. For example, costs rise at all levels of activity when an administered price rises. Since such a price increase is seldom reversed, it raises future costs and is factored into the pricing of sticky-price goods today. The definition of potential output then also has to be changed. An economy is at its potential if second-round supply shocks are keeping inflation above a threshold (Goyal and Arora 2013).

When cost-push is zero, only current and future demand causes inflation. The CB can then vary interest rates to set excess demand to zero for all time and lower inflation with no cost in terms of output, which remains at its potential. A fall in output is required to lower inflation only if cost-push is positive. So a short-run trade-off between inflation and output variability arises only if there is positive cost-push inflation unless backward-looking behavior is extensive. The flatter the supply curve, however, the greater the output cost of a given disinflation.[12] Even if the AS is flat, to the extent EMs can mitigate the cost-push factors pushing up average costs and the AS, output costs of disinflation can be reduced.

In mature economies, the modern macroeconomic approach focuses on employment. In this class of models, labor is the key output driver (Woodford

[11] The Lucas critique of early Keynesian models was that since the IS-LM and PC were not derived from individual behavior, parameters could change with policy shocks, making the relationships unreliable for the analysis of policy.

[12] IMF (2013) finds that the AS curve has become flat in AEs. The reason is better anchored inflation expectations. The reason in EMs is elastic output. But volatile exogenous cost shocks shift up the AS in EMs.

Fig. 1.1 Aggregate demand and supply

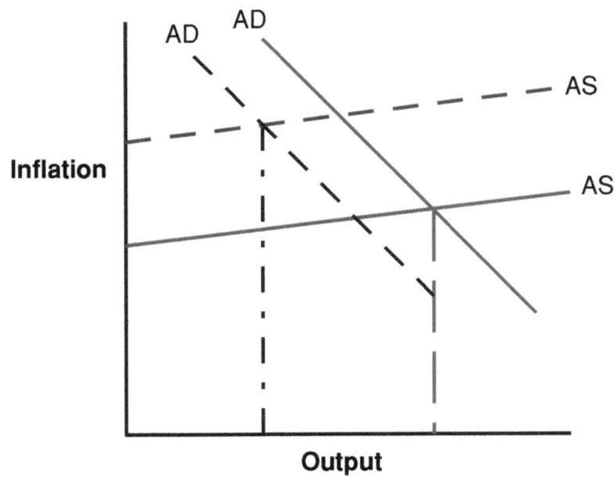

2003). Capital is a produced means of production. Moreover, in an open economy, resource bottlenecks are easier to alleviate. But even while following that approach, in EMs, low productive labor in the large informal sector is treated as structurally unemployed. But once a populous EM crosses a critical threshold and high catch-up growth is established, higher labor mobility blurs the distinction between formal and informal sectors. Some part of the hitherto structurally unemployed are better treated as cyclically unemployed. A macroeconomics of the aggregate economy becomes both necessary and feasible. In labor-surplus economies established on a catch-up growth path, capital is available to equip labor and raise its productivity. Savings rise with growth, and capital flows in with greater openness. In India, moreover, the demographic structuredevelopment implies that 12 million youth are expected to enter the labor force each year through the 2010s (Goyal and Arora 2013).

So the aggregate supply (AS) or PC is elastic, especially in the longer run (Fig. 1.1). But inefficiencies, distortions, and cost shocks push aggregate supply upward, over an entire output range, rather than only at full employment, since that is not reached at current output ranges and output is elastic. Average cost rises rather than cost at the margin. The AS becomes vertical only as the economy matures and full productive employment is reached.

With such a structure, demand has a greater impact on output and supply on inflation. This is the sense in which the economy is supply-constrained (Goyal 2011a, 2012). This framework differs from the early idea that output cannot be demand-determined in a developing economy because of supply bottlenecks (Rao 1952). Here, output is demand-determined, but the supply side raises costs. It also differs from the structural school that requires a disaggregated structure where industrial output is demand–determined, but agricultural output is fixed at a time period. The difference arises because in an open economy supply, bottlenecks are easier to alleviate (Goyal 2004). The share of agriculture shrinks and agricultural commodities can also be imported, although the price depends on the exchange rate and world prices. A depreciation of the currency is one of the forces raising costs and pushing up the supply curve.

Given low per capita incomes, and the large share of food in the consumption basket, the food price wage cycle is an important mechanism propagating supply shocks and creating inflationary expectations. If markets are perfectly clearing and prices and wages are flexible, then a fall in one price balances a rise in another with no effect on the aggregate price level. But prices and wages rise more easily than they fall. So, a rise in a critical price raises wages and therefore other prices, generating inflation. Some relative prices, among them food prices and the exchange rate, have more of such an impact. Food prices are critical for inflation in India, and since international food inflation now influences domestic, the exchange rate becomes relevant. Other types of populist policies that give short-term subsidies but raise hidden or indirect costs also contribute to cost-push. For example, poor infrastructure and public services increase costs (Goyal 2012).

Political pressures from farmers push up farm support prices, with consumption subsidies also going up. But these are inadequate due to corruption and failures of targeting, so nominal wages rise with a lag, pushing up costs and generating second-round inflation from a temporary supply shock. This political economy indexes wages informally to food price inflation. Political support also raises indexed informal wages formally through minimum wage and employment schemes such as MGNREGS.

A study (Goyal and Baikar 2014) of the high-inflation period 2007–2012 showed that a sharp rise in real rural wages took place despite low growth because of the exceptional rise in food prices and the large share of government expenditure directed to rural areas that helped raise social norms of expected minimum wages. Rather than a specific scheme, general government expenditures played a role. Repeated food price shocks kept nominal wage growth high, but there was not a wage–price spiral. One link of the spiral from food prices to wages was strong, but the further link from wages to rural prices was weak. Although expected food inflation affected nominal wage growth, wages did not affect rural prices. The greater effect of food prices on wages compared to wages on food prices suggests that there was some rise in productivity. More than wages, multiple supply shocks impacted food prices—starting with the international food price shocks of 2007, monsoonfailures in 2009, and episodes of sharp rupee depreciation in 2008, 2011, and 2013. So food prices were critical. Despite increase in productivity, essential complementary policies to remove marketing restrictions and other structural impediments in agriculture were missing.

Rigorous empirical tests based on structural vector autoregression (VAR), time series causality,generalized method of moments (GMM) regressions of aggregate demand (AD) and aggregate supply (AS), and calibrations in a dynamic stochastic general equilibrium (DSGE) model for the Indian economy support the elastic longer-run supply and the dominance of supply shocks (Goyal 2005, 2008, 2011b, 2012). The sustained food inflation since 2008 did lead to some analysis of supply-side factors (Gokarn 2011, Mohanty 2010). Joshi and Little (1994) have long argued that supply-side responses have been neglected in Indian macroeconomic policy.

Under a positive cost shock, forcing an immediate reduction in inflation would have a cost in terms of output foregone, which is especially high with the above structure of AD and AS. But, even with these structural inflation drivers, monetary accommodation is required to sustain inflation and inflation expectations. With such a structure, if some type of inflation targeting is to be considered, it should be flexible inflation forecast targeting with a positive weight to output stabilization. This can anchor expectations at minimum output costs.

To apply inflation targeting, the CB has to first establish that it can reasonably forecast inflation. In an EM, a monetary conditions' index can be a precursor or complement to more formal inflation forecasting. It is a weighted set of variables that affect aggregate demand. The set and weights vary across countries but include money and credit aggregates, short-term interest rates, exchange rates and their fluctuations, direct measures of domestic inflation, commodity prices, wages, and even some real variables such as capacity utilization. The multiple indicator regime India moved to in 1998 was of this type. This can naturally graduate to flexible inflation forecast targeting by more clearly indicating how these variables affect the forecast.

Greater model uncertainty, and more backward-looking behavior in EMs, leads to making less than full use of forward-looking behavior in designing policy, in order to collect more information as well as lower asset–price volatility. The short-term interest rate mainly affects capital flows, exchange rates, and other asset prices. It is the long-term interest rates that affect aggregate demand. Smoothing short-term interest rates can lower volatility in asset prices and yet allow the CB to directly affect demand through the long-term rate. If the short-term interest rate is expected to rise in the future, for example, the long-term rate will rise even more. So the long-term rate can be affected with a smaller current change in the short-term rate. But markets need to be surprised sometimes to prevent overleverage and excessive risk-taking.

With flexible inflation forecast or zone targeting, sharp changes in interest rates are not required. In an EM, there is a high degree of uncertainty attached to potential growth. It changes more as reforms raise efficiency and the share of volatile private investment rises. With a flexible target, changes in potential growth can be allowed to reveal themselves. If inflation does not rise even as output exceeds the expected potential, the potential must have risen. First-round effects of supply shocks can be excluded from the forecast target. Escape clauses can be built in for temporary supply shocks. Core inflation exempts volatile prices such as food and oil and therefore captures persistent demand-driven inflation the CB can affect. However, headline inflation impacts the consumer and directly affects household expectations. If it becomes persistent, it cannot be ignored. But if headline inflation is targeted, policy flexibility becomes even more important.

In a small open economy, monetary policy transmission depends also on the exchange rate channel. The lag from the exchange rate to consumer prices is the shortest (Svensson 2000), especially if commodities dominate imports. In a typical EM, the effect of the exchange rate on inflation and capital flows and its role as an asset–price dominate. In these circumstances, letting the nominal exchange rate vary in a target band around the real exchange rate can help smooth the nominal interest rate instrument. If two-way movement of the nominal exchange rate is synchronized with temporary supply shocks, and the exchange rate appreciates with a negative supply shock, food and intermediate goods price inflation is contained. This serves to preempt the effect of temporary supply shocks on the domestic price–wage process[13]. Building in a rule whereby there is an automatic announced response to an expected supply shock avoids the tendency to do nothing until it becomes necessary to over-react. Actions linked to exogenous shocks avoid moral hazard.

At the very least, managed floating would prevent sharp depreciations that add to inflationary pressures. In a managed float intervention, smoothing net foreign currency demand and signaling can all be used to reverse deviations of the exchange rate from equilibriumor prevent excessive depreciation, thus reducing present and future volatility and the pressure to raise interest rates in response to inflation. To the extent nominal exchange rate movements reduce inflation, the policy rate can respond less to inflation and focus more on deviations from potential output. Even inflation targeting Brazil manages its currency to support an inflation target.

Two-way movementof the exchange rate also encourages hedging, thus reducing risk and developing foreign exchange markets. Variation of a managed float in a band not less than ten percent prevents riskless "puts" against the CB, since then there is a substantial risk of loss if the expected movement does not materialize. Such a band worked in the European exchange rate mechanism. The central value need not be announced and can change with inflation differentials in order to prevent real over- or undervaluation. It thus keeps the real exchange rate near equilibrium values, preventing large and distorting deviation from fundamentals that can arise easily in thin markets. There is evidence that while currency crises adversely affect trade, limited fluctuation in exchange rates does not have a large effect on trade. If limited volatility helps prevent crises and lower interest rates, it may even benefit trade.

EMs typically have less information and more uncertainty, so a variety of signals can be effective. Different types of research-based estimates of equilibrium exchange ratescan contribute to focusing market expectations, even without a commitment to defend the estimates. In addition to the inflation-differential-based REER published currently, a fundamental value of the rupee based on factors such as unit labor costs and real wages could be published, to help anchor long-term market expectations. Intervention must not be one-sided and has to be strategic. Timing of intervention is very important and must be based on market intelligence covering net open positions, order flow, bid-ask spreads (when one-sided positions dominate dealers withdraw from supplying liquidity and spreads rise), turnover, and share of interbank trades.

Thus, forward-looking monetary policy can use its knowledge of structure to abort the inflationary process. During a catch-up period of rapid productivity growth, potential output exceeds output. As supply shocks are the dominant source of inflation, optimal policy should aim to achieve an inflation target only over the

---

[13] In typical closed economy structuralist models, agricultural markets were price clearing with quantities given, while quantities adjusted in non-agricultural markets. Therefore, money supply could affect food prices. But in an open economy, agricultural supplies are not fixed even in the short period since imports are possible (Goyal 2004). Now, the exchange rate affects food prices (Goyal 2010).

medium term by which time temporary supply shocks have petered out or been countered by exchange rate policy, changes in tax rates, or supply-side improvements. Flexible inflation targeting itself will prevent the inflationary wage–price expectations from setting in that can imply a permanent upward shift in the supply curve from a temporary supply shock. Monetary policy has to tighten sharply only if there is excess demand.

But in the international experience, inflation targeting has been combined with an independent CB. Is this prerequisite satisfied in India?

1.4 Institutions

In a democracy, CBs are responsible for monetary and financial stability, but the government is subject to the pressures of election. Therefore, the latter often forces the CB to try to raise output and employment. Once workers have made their work decisions based on expected wages, if the CB creates surprise inflation, this lowers real wages and unemployment since firms are then willing to employ larger numbers. Workers are tricked into working for lower wages. But over time, such behavior becomes anticipated and higher nominal wage adjustments are built in, so there is only excess inflation, with no decrease in unemployment. This is known as the inflation bias, and a large literature on it explores the structure of institutions such as independence of a CB or appointment of a conservative central banker that can allow the CB to resist potential pressure. Bureaucrats are expected to be able to take a longer view compared to politicians since their reputation, not winning elections, is their prime objective.

But in a poor populous democracy without full indexation of wages and prices, inflation hurts the poor who have the most votes. Therefore, democratic accountability also acts to force the CB to keep inflation low, unlike in mature economies. It is the fiscal authority that is tempted to make excess populist expenditures, forcing the CB to accommodate fiscal needs, while using distorting administrative measures, including price and credit controls, to keep inflation low. India's post-independence monetary history demonstrates these features.

A democratically accountable central banker in a developing democracy would anyway keep inflation low, so if stricter rules restrain fiscal populism, the CB can focus less on inflation and more on growth. More autonomy to the CB can, without changes in the rules of the game through fiscal reform, lead to higher interest rates that increase the burden of public debt and have a high output cost. India's post-reform experience demonstrates this aspect also. CBs are accountable if they are partially independent. Too much independence can reduce democratic accountability. One way to prevent this is to allow instrument but not goal independence. The government sets the social goal, but the CB is free to implement it using its professional competence and knowledge (Goyal 2002, 2007). In 2014, opinion in India seems to be converging to a medium-term inflation target set by Parliament that the RBI would implement.

1.4.1 Precedents and Path Dependence

Preindependence, the discussion preceding the setting up of the RBI emphasized the importance of setting up an institution free of political influence.[14] There was a debate, but even those on opposite sides agreed on the importance of at least instrument independence. Under the preindependence RBI Act, the RBI was obligated to carry out the responsibilities laid on it by statute. It was nationalized at independence, but under the constitution and the division of responsibilities, if the RBI said no to the finance minister, the government would have to go to Parliament, which could assert some discipline.

But the early view of planning as a national goal established precedents and procedures that vitiated the autonomy of the RBI. The initial jockeying between the RBI and the Ministry of Finance[15] made it clear that the RBI was to be regarded as a department of the government. Monetary policy was another instrument to achieve national goals. The RBI lost even instrument independence.

> For the Reserve Bank of India therefore, short-term monetary policy meant not merely managing clearly identified variables such as the price level or the exchange rate, but doing so consistent with supporting a given Plan effort. ...The practical necessities of decision making under multiple constraints often led to the adoption, sometimes against the better judgment of its officers if not always of the Bank, of measures which created bigger problems in the longer-term than the more immediate ones they helped resolve. As the logic of decision-making became endogenized in the form of precedents and institutional evolution, the course was set for departures which however small or partial in the beginning, exercised over a period of time a tangible influence on the overall effectiveness of the Bank's monetary policy (Balachandran 1998, p. 10).

An example of such a precedent was the RBI's agreement to the government's January 1955 proposal to create ad hoc treasury bills to maintain the government's cash balances at INR 50 crores or above, thus making soft credit available to the government in unlimited quantities. With the aid of this facility, the issue of ad hocs rose during the second plan. The government also reduced safeguards restricting currency expansion.

The RBI's early conservative CB stance changed by the second plan to one that supported the government's financing requirements. By 1967, the heterodox 1951 Yojana Bhavan perspective on monetary policy had become the orthodox RBI view—it had adopted and internalized the opposite government view. Where the government pulled the RBI found itself following.

---

[14] The cynics view was that this was to ensure the country remained solvent and could continue to make payments to the British (see Anjaneyulu et al. 2010).

[15] In the mid-1950s, Rama Rau, the then governor of the RBI, resigned because of pressures from the Finance Minister TT Krishnamachari. The latter imposed a steep rise in the stamp duty of bills that effectively destroyed the bill market that Rama Rau was keen to develop.

The government wanted lower interest rates given its large borrowings, and this made it difficult for the RBI to raise rates.[16] It early showed itself to be susceptible to pressures to support government borrowing through Gsecs. Even in 1951, banks were given an exemption from showing capital losses from their holdings of Gsecs on their balance sheets (Balachandran 1998, p. 55). As manager of the government debt, the RBI generally sought to support the government borrowing program.

Independence depended also on personalities. Governor Bhattacharyya managed to raise the bank rate over 1963–1965, for the first time after 1957. In the early 1950s, under Rama Rau, the bank rate used to be changed, and there were attempts to develop an active bill market for short-term financing. In the 1920s and 1930s, an active bill market had provided seasonal finance.

In 1962, Iengar pointed out four areas of conflict between the government and the RBI: interest rate policy, deficit financing, cooperative credit policies, and management of substandard banks. The RBI had worked toward larger-sized financially viable rural cooperatives that would have eliminated the middleman. But the government destroyed these initiatives by insisting on village-level cooperatives and on using rural credit as patronage. There were dissenting voices to the path the country and its institutions were taking (Chandavarkar 2005). An article in the Hindu commenting on an early RBI committee pointed to the dangers of entrenching State control and distrust of the individual (Balachandran 1998, p. 241). It was feared that the government's top-down approach toward the cooperative movementwould reduce self-reliance and increase dependence on the State.

In 1967, Governor Jha stated that given the plans, it was not possible to control aggregate credit. So the RBI should focus on controlling sectoral credit to achieve its twin goals of development and stability (Balachandran 1998, p. 730). Worried about the effect of steady monetization of deficits on the money supply, the bank fought for and got additional powers in 1956, by expanding section 42 of the RBI Act, to give it control over banks' cash reserves. A 1962 modification gave it the power to vary the cash reserve ratio (CRR) between 3 and 15 % of scheduled bank's demand and time liabilities. The liquidity provisions of the Banking Companies Act were also changed and termed the statutory liquidity ratio (SLR). It was now possible to use these to divert bank resources for government financing, while reducing money supply.

The economy had always been vulnerable to the monsoon. In the early 1970s, oil shocks were a new kind of supply shock. The government and the RBI were afraid of high inflation. The new instruments enabled a squeeze on money and credit in response to supply shocks, which intensified the demand recession that followed. This discouraged growth and productivity increases that would have lowered inflation from the cost side.

The stagnation in the economy, rising government indebtedness, and scarcity of foreign exchange precipitated a balance of payment crisis in the early 1990s. More openness was regarded as a solution. This was the way the rest of the world was

---

[16] In 1964–1965, Finance Minister TT Krishnamachari even claimed for the government the right to announce bank rate changes when Parliament was in session. But Bhattacharyya was able to defend the bank's right to announce the bank rate and was also able to raise rates. Even such "symbolic" rights are important for autonomy (Balachandran 1998, pp. 741).

going and was also in line with current dominant global ideas. But more openness required more credible institutions. Poor fiscal finances had precipitated many outflows and currency crises in EMs. Therefore, liberalizing reforms in the 1990s strengthened the autonomy of the RBI compared to the government. Ad hoc treasury bills and automatic monetization of the deficits were stopped in the 1990s. The ways and means advance (WMA) system was started in 1997. Primary issues of government securities no longer devolved on the RBI. From April 1, 2006, the RBI no longer participated in the primary auction of government securities.

1.4.2 Strengthening Institutions

A Fiscal Responsibility and Budget Management(FRBM) Act was enacted by Parliament in 2003. The rules accompanying the FRBM Act required the Center to reduce the fiscal deficit to 3 % of GDP and eliminate revenuedeficit by March 31, 2008. The budget was to each year place before Parliament the Medium-Term Fiscal Policy, Fiscal Policy Strategy, and Macroeconomic Framework statements. Monetization of the deficit was banned, but there were no restrictions on OMOs. Any deviations from the FRBM Act require the permission of Parliament. If the targets were not met, a pro rata cut on all expenditures was to be imposed without protecting capital expenditure. There was also a ceiling on guarantees. But the ceilings were allowed to be exceeded during "national security or national calamity or such other exceptional grounds as the Central Government may specify." This implied that the government could legislate itself out of the commitments, as it did after the Lehman crisis when it deviated from the mandated consolidation path, requesting the 13th Finance Commission to set out a new path.

The FRBM Act brought down only reported deficits. The GFC exposed the inadequate attention paid to incentives and escape clauses in formulating the Act. Loopholes were found to maintain the letter of the law even while violating its spirit. Off-budget liabilities such as oil bonds were used to subsidize some petroleum products. Targets were mechanically achieved, compressing essential expenditure on infrastructure, health, and education, while maintaining populist vote-catching subsidies. The Act requires to be reframed to improve incentives for compliance. Expenditure caps that bite especially on transfers, while protecting productive expenditure, will create better incentives. They will also moderate the temptation to raise expenditure when actual or potential revenues rise. These are examples of automatic non-discretionary stabilizers. With phased caps on spending rather than on the deficit, the latter could increase in case of economic slowdown when revenues fall, thus allowing automatic countercyclical macrostabilization and increasing the political feasibility of the scheme. The deficit should vary over the cycle; that is, it should be cyclically adjusted.

In the Indian context, especially urgent are detailed expenditure targets for individual ministries and levels of government, as part of improved accounting, including shifts from cash to accrual-based accounts. These should change the composition of government expenditure toward productive expenditure that improves human, social, and physical capital and therefore the supply response. Essential transfers must be better targeted to reduce waste, and the effectiveness of government expenditure improved. Any permanent rise in expenditure must be linked to a specific tax source. Incentives the 12th Finance Commission gave for States to adopt an FRBM worked very well, leading to large improvements in State finances. The 13th Finance Commission brought in some cyclical adjustment but did not build in better incentives for compliance at the Center.

A more credible FRBM will allow better fiscal–monetary coordination. To use Woodford's (2003) terminology, an active monetary policy can support growth if fiscal policy passively follows the path of consolidation. They can then switch positions during a crisis with monetary policy passively supporting active fiscal stimuli. The more usual combination in post-reform India, as the RBI gained greater independence, was for both to be active, which harmed growth, as overall monetary tightening sought to compensate for fiscal giveaways. Sharp rise in policy and other liberalized interest rates periodically lowered growth after the reforms. When Indian interest rates did fall after 2000, despite high government deficits and aggressive sterilization, because international interest rates fell, growth was stimulated. But in 2011, and in 2013, when policy rates peaked, industrial demand and output fell sharply, while populist transfers financed by the high FD maintained demand for food where there were supply and marketing bottlenecks. Thus, government spending maintained inflation, while monetary tightening reduced industrial growth. Demand in the modern sector is the most interest sensitive.

The composition of government spending has major effects. If fiscal legislation successfully shifts public expenditure toward public services that build private capacity, then openness gives an opportunity for monetary authorities to lower Indian real interest rates closer to world levels. Since accountability, in a democratic policy, forces the CB to keep inflation low, a weak constraint on the CB—such as medium-term inflation zone targeting supported by supply-side action—would be credible. This would stabilize inflation expectations, lowering the cost of disinflation. Thus, measures to change aggregate demand would be required only if inflation forecasts are outside the zone; otherwise, productivity improvements can be allowed to decrease inflation in their own time, under expanding potential output. This gives sufficient discretion to smooth policy rates and yet achieve the desired objectives (Goyal 2002). Pressures to reduce the FD also come from internationalrating agencies, since a downgrade automatically leads to outflows. This possibility forced a fiscal contraction in 2013, after the post-GFC fiscal stimulus had expanded deficits.

1.4.3 Openness, Markets, and CB Autonomy

Threats to the autonomy of CBs come not only from the government, but also from free capital flows. The Mundell–Fleming model tells us that with perfect capital mobility, static expectations, and a fixed exchange rate, monetary autonomy is lost. Monetary policymakers often refer to this impossible trinity, indicating their helplessness before waves of foreign inflows and the increasing dominance of the market. But internationally, and in India, the potential impact of monetary policy has increased with the reforms. First, exchange rate regimes in most countries, and especially in EMs like India, are somewhere between a perfect fix and a perfect float. Even partial flexibility of exchange rates gives some monetary autonomy. Second, the absence of complete capital account convertibility (as in India) opens up more degrees of freedom. Consider a triangle where the bottom two cornersrepresent a fixed and a floating exchange rate and the line between them depicts the whole range of intermediate regimes. The upper point is a closed capital account, so that in approaching the bottom line convertibility, gradually increases until perfect capital mobility is reached on the line. Therefore, the impossible trinity is only one point of the triangle. Everywhere else there is varying degrees of monetary autonomy. So, in the final analysis, more openness actually increased degrees of freedom for policy. The loss in freedom from capital flows was not large enough to nullify greater freedom from fiscal dominance.

Deeper markets with greater interest sensitivity make monetary policy more effective. To the extent behavior is forward-looking, taking markets into confidence, or strategic revelation of information, can sometimes help achieve policy objectives. But markets factor in news and the expected policy stance, making it difficult for policy to go against market expectations. So, in a sense, monetary policy also loses autonomy to free markets. The latter demand transparency and like predictability. But after the GFC, it is recognized that price discovery in markets can deviate from fundamentals. Market efficiency does not always hold, and markets do not satisfy rational expectations.

Markets can get caught in a trap of self-fulfilling expectations around unsustainable overleveraged positions. So it is necessary at times to focus expectations around better outcomes. This may involve surprising markets—creating news. Blinder et al. (2008) show that the two ways in which communicationmakes monetary policy more effective are by creating news and by reducing uncertainty. Surprise can be compatible with more transparency if it is linked to random shocks to which the system is subject—then, communication enhances news (Goyal et al. 2009).

Thus, free markets also reduce CB autonomy, but the global crisis has resulted in giving institutions and regulators some degrees of freedom. It has also led to a reassessment of the CB's objective beyond a narrow focus on inflation targeting. Financial stabilityhas been recognized as a major objective. As the regulator of banks, the RBI has always given priority to financial stability and has effectively used macroprudential instruments. These are now being recognized worldwide as necessary complements to the interest rate instrument.

Table 1.7 Annual average macrostatistics in tenures of Reserve Bank Governors

Governor	From	To	Tenure period	Monetary policy			Real GDP growth
				RM	M3	Inflation	
Shri H.V.R. Iengar	Mar 1957	Feb 1962	1957–1958 to 1961–1962	6.11	8.21	3.52	3.76
Shri P.C.Bhattacharya	Mar 1962	Jul 1967	1962–1963 to 1966–1967	8.16	9.93	7.28	2.42
Shri L.K. Jha	Jun 1967	May 1970	1967–1968 to 1969–1970	7.97	12.23	8.58	5.73
Shri Jagannathan	Jun 1970	May 1975	1970–1971 to 1974–1975	12.93	15.44	12.67	2.3
Shri I.G. Patel	Dec-77	Sep 1982	1977–1978 to 1982–1983	15.57	17.55	9.13	4.03
Shri Manmohan Singh	Sep 1982	Jan 1985	1983–1984 to 1984–1985	23.46	18.60	7[b]	6
Shri R.N. Malhotra	Feb 1985	Dec 1990	1985–1986 to 1990–1991	16.54	17.14	7.26	5.93
Shri S. Venkatiramanan	Dec 1990	Dec 1992	1991–1992 to 1992–1993	12.35	17.05	11.9	3.2
Dr. C. Rangarajan	Dec 1992	Nov 1997	1993–1994 to 1997–1998	15.64	17.72	7.6	6.62[a]
Dr. Bimal Jalan	Nov 1997	Sept 2003	1998–1999 to 2002–2003	10.28	15.42	4.66	5.38
Dr. Y.V. Reddy	Sept 2003	Sept 2008	2003–2004 to 2007–2008	20.43	18.58	5.29	9.01
Dr. D. Subbarao	Sept 2008	Sept 2013	2008–2009 to 2012–2013	10.5	15.9	7.6 (10.1)	6.5

Source For the period after 1970–1971, Reserve Bank, before that reserve money (RM) is from IMF and Financial Statistics, and inflation and output from NAS and CSO

Note The last four columns give growth rates

The output figures from [a] refer to the new series of the CSO, with base 1993–1994, prior to that the base was 1980–1981. The inflation series are derived from the Wholesale Price Index, before [b] the base is 1970–1971, after it is 1981–1982, from 1993–1994, it is that year, and for the last row, it is 2004–2005 for both GDP at market prices and WPI. The term in brackets gives average CPI inflation, which was much higher in this period

1.4.4 Bank Governors and Delegation in India

One of the measures suggested in the literature to increase independence is to delegate authority to a conservative central banker, who will then impose own preferences on the growth inflation trade-off (Vasudevan 2005).

Table 1.7 shows that growth, inflation, and monetary policy have differed in the tenures of various Reserve Bank governors. The overall direction may have been dictated by the preferences of the elected government, given lack of constitutional autonomy. But the delegated agent, or the Governor, has been able to make a difference. The divergence in performance in the regimes of different governors suggests that their preferences affected growth rates. Second, governors in whose regime growth was higher delivered lower inflation. Cost shocks normally sparked higher inflation, but the monetary response affected growth and future inflation. Short-run sharp inflation caused by supply shocks was controlled through a fall in demand, but it harmed long-term growth. The clear differences in regimes suggest that governors whose policies discouraged recovery in growth ended up with higher inflation also (Goyal 2007). The two governors with the highest rates of growth of reserve money, Dr. Manmohan Singh and Dr. Reddy, also had local maxima in rates of growth and minima in rates of inflation.

In Chap. 2, we turn to the policy actions emanating from this institutional structure and the outcomes produced, given the elasticities of AD-AS.

References

Anjaneyulu D, Singh D, Srinivasa Raghavan TCA (2010) Untitled ms, History of monetary policy 1900 to Independence

Balachandran A (1998) The Reserve Bank of India, 1951–1967. University Press, Oxford

Balakrishna P (1994) How best to model inflation in India. J Policy Model 677–683

Blanchard O, D'Aricca G, Mauro P (2010) Rethinking monetary policy. IMF. http://www.imf.org/external/pubs/ft/spn/2010/spn1003.pdf. Accessed Jan 2014

Blinder AS, Ehrmann M, Fratzscher M, Haan JD, Jansen DJ (2008) Central bank communication and monetary policy: a survey of theory and evidence. J Econ Lit 46(4):910–945

Brahmananda, PR (2001) Money income prices in 19th century India. Himalaya Publishing House, Mumbai

Chandavarkar A (2005) Towards an independent federal Reserve Bank of India. Econ Political Weekly 3837–3845

Chitre VS (1986) Quarterly prediction of reserve money multiplier and money stock in India. Artha Vijnana 28:1–123

Clarida R, Gali J, Gertler M (1999) The science of monetary policy: a new Keynesian perspective. J Econ Lit 37(4):1661–1707

Clarida R, Gali J, Gertler M (2001) Optimal monetary policy in closed versus open economies: an integrated approach. Am Econ Rev 91(2):248–252

Dash S, Goyal A (2000) The money supply process in India: identification, analysis and estimation. Indian Econ J 48(1):90–102

Friedman M, Schwartz AJ (1971) A monetary history of the United States: 1867–1960. Princeton University Press, Princeton
Gokarn S (2011) The price of protein. Macroecon Financ Emerg Market Econ 4(2):327–335
Goodhart C (2007) The continuing muddles of monetary theory: a steadfast refusal to face facts. (mimeo) Financial Markets Group, London School of Economics
Goyal A (2002) Coordinating monetary and fiscal policies: a role for rules? In: Parikh KS, Radhakrishna R (eds) India Development Report, Chap. 1.1. IGIDR and Oxford University Press, New Delhi
Goyal A (2003) Budgetary processes: a political economy perspective. In Morris S (ed) India infrastructure report 2003, public expenditure allocation and accountability, Chapter 2.2. 3iNetwork and Oxford University Press, New Delhi
Goyal A (2004) The impact of structure and openness on the causal ordering of interest, inflation and exchange rates. J Quant Econ 2(2):223–242 (Special Issue in Memory of M J Manohar Rao)
Goyal A (2005) Reducing endogenous amplification of shocks from capital flows in developing countries.GDN project report. http://www.gdnet.org/pdf2/gdn_library/global_research_projects/macro_low_income/Goyal.pdf. Accessed in 2010
Goyal A (2007) Tradeoffs, delegation and fiscal-monetary coordination in a developing economy. Indian Econ Rev 42(2):141–164
Goyal A (2008) Incentives from exchange rate regimes in an institutional context. J Quant Econ 6(1&2):101–121
Goyal (2010) Inflationary pressures in South Asia. Asia-Pacific Develop J 17(2):1–42
Goyal A (2011a) Exchange rate regimes and macroeconomic performance in South Asia. In: Jha R (ed) Routledge handbook on South Asian economies. pp 143–155. Oxon and NY: Routledge
Goyal A (2011b) A general equilibrium open economy model for emerging markets: monetary policy with a dualistic labor market. Econ Model 28(2):1392–1404
Goyal A (2012)Propagation mechanisms in inflation: governance as key. In S. Mahendra Dev (ed) India Development Report 2012, Chap. 3. IGIDR and Oxford University Press, New Delhi, pp 32–46
Goyal A (2014) Introduction and overview. In: Goyal A (ed) The Oxford handbook of the Indian economy in the 21st century. Oxford University Press, New Delhi. Forthcoming
Goyal A, Arora S (2013). Inferring India's potential growth and policy stance. J Quant Econ 11(1&2):60–83
Goyal A, Baikar AK (2014) Psychology, cyclicality or social programs: rural wage and inflation dynamics in India. IGIDR working paper no. WP-2014-014. http://www.igidr.ac.in/pdf/publication/WP-2014-014.pdf
Goyal A, Nair RA, Samantaraya A (2009) Monetary policy, forex markets, and feedback under uncertainty in an opening economy. Development Research Group, Department of Economic Analysis and Policy, Reserve Bank of India, Mumbai, Study No. 32. http://rbidocs.rbi.org.in/rdocs/Publications/PDFs/DRGMP030909.pdf. Accessed in 2010
Gupta SB (1976) Factors affecting money supply: critical evaluation of Reserve Bank's analysis. Econ Political Weekly 11:117–128
International Monetary Fund (IMF) (2013) The dog that didn't bark: has inflation been muzzled or was it just sleeping? In: World economic outlook: hopes, realities, risks (Chap. 3)
Jadhav N (1990) Monetary modeling of the Indian economy: asurvey.RBI Occas Pap 11:83–152
Joshi V, Little IMD (1994) India: macroeconomics and political economy. 1964–1991. Oxford University Press, Delhi
Krishnamurthy K, Pandit VN (1985) Macroeconomic modeling of the Indian economy: studies on inflation and growth. Hindustan Publishing Corporation, New Delhi
Mohanty D (2010) Perspectives on inflation in India. Speech given at the Bankers Club, Chennai, 28 Sept
Nachane DM (2003) P R Brahmananda; Obituary. Econ Political Weekly 870–872
Nachane DM, Ray D (1989) The money multiplier: are examination of Indian evidence. Indian Econ J 37:56–73

Pendharkar VG, Narasimham M (1966) Recent evolution of monetary policy in India. Reserve Bank India Bull 340–361
Radcliffe Report (1958–1959) Report of the Committee on the Working of the Monetary System. http://www.jstor.org/stable/138787
Rakshit M (2009) Money and finance in the Indian economy, vol 2. Oxford University Press, New Delhi
Rangarajan C, Singh A (1984) Reserve money: Concepts and implications for India. Occasional papers, Reserve Bank of India
Rao VKRV (1952) Investment, income and the multiplier in an underdeveloped economy. The Indian Economic Review, February, reprinted in Agarwala AN and Singh SP (eds) The economics of underdevelopment. Oxford University Press, Oxford, pp 205–218, 1958
Rao MJM, Singh B (1995) Analytical foundations of financial programming and growth oriented adjustment. DRG study, DEAP, RBI, Bombay
Rao DC, Venkatachalam TR, Vasudevan A (1981) A short-term model to forecast monetary aggregates: some interim results.RBI Occas Pap 2:113–140
RBI (Reserve Bank of India) (1985) Report of the committee to review the working of the monetary system. (S. Chakravarty, Chariman), Bombay
Reserve Bank of India (RBI) (1987) Report of the working group on the money market (N. Vaghul, Chairman), Bombay
Reserve Bank of India (RBI) (1991) Report of the committee on the financial system (Chairman: M. Narasimham)
Singh A, Shetty SL, Venktachalam TR (1982) Monetary policy in India: issues and evidence. Suppl RBI Occas Pap 3:1–133
Svensson LEO (2000) Open-economy inflation targeting. J Int Econ 50:155–183
Vakil CN, Brahmananda PR (1956) Planning for an expanding economy: accumulation employment and technical progress in underdeveloped countries. Vora and Co, Bombay
Vasudevan A (1977) Demand for money in India: a survey of literature. Reserve Bank Staff Occasional Papers, 2 June
Vasudevan A (2005) On central bank reforms. Econ Political Weekly 40(42) Oct 15. Available at http://beta.epw.in/newsItem/comment/61761/
Woodford M (2003) Interest and prices: foundations of a theory of monetary policy. Princeton University Press, Princeton

Chapter 2
Policy Actions and Outcomes

Abstract The SIIO paradigm is developed further showing how the structure, ideas, and institutions analyzed in Chap. 1 affected Indian monetary policy outcomes. An aggregate demand–supply framework derived from forward-looking optimization subject to Indian structural constraints is able to explain growth and inflation outcomes given policy actions. Exogenous supply shocks are used to identify policy shocks and isolate their effects. It turns out policy was often procyclical and sometimes excessively tight when the common understanding is there was a large monetary overhang. But the three factors that cause a loss of monetary autonomy—governments, markets, and openness—are moderating each other. Open markets moderate fiscal profligacy and dominance. Global crises moderate markets and openness as they encourage greater caution. More congruence between ideas and structure is improving institutions and contributing to India's better performance.

Keywords Aggregate demand–supply framework · Policy shocks · Growth and inflation outcomes · Openness · Markets · Fiscal dominance · Monetary autonomy

2.1 The Historical Trajectory

Early monetary policy was geared to support planned expenditures and government deficits.[1] During an agricultural shock, monetary policy would initially support drought relief and then tighten just as the lagged demand effects of an agricultural

[1] The analysis in this section draws on RBI publications including monetary policy statements, speeches by RBI governors and data available on the RBI's website www.rbi.org.in and is updated from some of my earlier publications.

A. Goyal, *History of Monetary Policy in India Since Independence*,
SpringerBriefs in Economics, DOI 10.1007/978-81-322-1961-3_2

slowdown were hitting industry. Administered oil and food prices were normally raised with a lag after monetary tightening brought inflation rates down. Macropolicy was thus procyclical, but pervasive administered prices limited volatility.

Severe drought and terms of trade shocks over 1965–1967 led to a fiscal tightening, with a cut in deficits and in public investment. Monetary policy following a credit-targeting approach was non-accommodating but not severe. Fiscal–monetary policies were closely linked, as the budget deficit was automatically financed. Severe monetary and fiscal measures followed the oil price plus agricultural supply shock over 1973–1975. In both cases, there was an unnecessary loss of output. A focus on sustaining supply would have been more effective. After the 1979–1980 oil shock, the cut in public investment and sharp monetary tightening was avoided. Recovery was rapid, but deficits and supply-side inadequacies were accumulating.

The relatively closed, import substitution and public investment-driven model of development followed and allowed macropolicy to be geared toward domestic requirements. As growth slowed, successful lobbying for subsidies could have led to increasing reliance on seignorage, since inflation is an easy-to-collect tax. But where more than half the population was below the poverty line and an even larger percentage had no social security or other protection against inflation, governments concerned with re-election could not afford high inflation. Thus, even though there was some positive seignorage revenue and automatic monetization of the deficit, commercial banks' ability to multiply the reserve base and create broad money was partially countered through draconian compulsory reserve and statutory liquidity requirements. This, together with administered prices, restrained inflation to politically acceptable levels.

Thus, political business cycles in India largely took the form of a cut in long-term development expenditures and interventions that distorted allocative efficiency, not of increased money creation. The future was sacrificed to satisfy populism in the present (Goyal 1999). These choices kept Indian inflation low by developing country standards, but it was chronic and higher than world inflation rates—and lowered feasible growth rates.

Since the 1970s, dominant development ideas changed to favor openness. In India, also the ill effects of controls were becoming obvious. Some liberalization started in the mid-1980s, but a major thrust for external openness came from the mid-1991 balance of payment crisis when foreign exchange reserves were down to 11 days of imports. The crisis, and a series of domestic scams, helped bring home the lesson that excessive interest controls and credit rationing were deleterious to growth and stability (Thorat 2010). It made possible the implementation of a number of pending committee reports.

Current account and partial capital accountliberalization, and a gradual move to more flexible exchange rates followed. Sequencing was well thought out. While controls continued on domestic portfolios, individual investments and debt inflows and institutional equity inflows were liberalized. Equity shares risks, while short-term debt flows create a heavy repayment burden in adverse times. On foreign debt, the sequence of relaxation favored commercial credit and longer-term debt

(Rangarajan 2002, 2004).[2] Major reforms were undertaken toward development of equity, forex money, and government security markets. These choices also reflected India's perceived comparative advantage in developing financial services. In comparison, China liberalized FDI much more than financial flows. India, however, had more domestic industry that wanted protection.

Accumulation of large public debt made the fiscal–monetary combination followed in the past unsustainable. The automatic monetization of the government deficit was stopped and auction-based market borrowing adopted for meeting the fiscal deficits. The repressed financial regime was dismantled, interest rates became more market determined, and the government began to borrow at market rates.

Bank liquidity funded speculative buying of stocks through repurchase transactions in government securities and bonds. These stock market scams led to further action to remove weaknesses such as lack of transparency in the market infrastructure for government securities, excess liquidity with public sector undertakings, inadequate internal controls due to low levels of computerization, and reliance on manual processing, which made the nexus between banks and brokers feasible. All administered interest rates were deregulated except the savings bank deposit rate. RBI initiated a delivery versus payment mechanism for netting and settlement of trades in government securities, leading to establishment of the Clearing Corporation of India (CCIL), a central counterparty to undertake guaranteed settlement for Gsecs, repos in Gsecs, and forex market trades.

As the bank regulator, RBI was an early pioneer in countercyclical prudential regulations that are being adopted worldwide after the GFC. Provisioning for bank housing and commercial real estate loans was raised as a countercyclical measure when Indian real estate prices rose after 2005. Accounting standards did not permit recognition of unrealized gains in equity or the profit and loss account, but unrealized losses had to be accounted. The relative conservativeness, without full marking-to-market requirements, reduced procyclical incentives. Banks were required to mark-to-market only investments held in trading categories. Exposures had conservative capital adequacy requirements under 2006 guidelines on securitization. Any profits on sale of assets to a special purpose vehicle were to be recognized only over the life of the pass-through certificates issued, not immediately on sale (Goyal 2009). These types of prudential regulations affect behavior while minimizing high transaction costs imposed by discretionary credit controls. They give a powerful additional weapon to prevent asset price bubbles, allowing the policy rate to focus on the real sector. In a more complex economy, credit controls become difficult for the regulator to operate, apart from the distortions they cause. By 1994, selective credit control operations had been largely phased out.

[2] In 2011, for example, an FII could invest up to 10 % of the total issued capital of an Indian company. The cap on aggregate debt flows from all FIIs together was 1.55 billion USD. This was increased to 30 billion to facilitate financing of the CAD. A given percentage of GDP implies very different absolute levels of inflows by the end of a period of rapid GDP growth—the absorptive capacity of the economy also rises. Inflows could only come through FIIs—individuals could not invest directly.

The basic objectives of monetary policy remained to be price stability and development, but in line with the recommendations of the Chakravarty Committee (RBI 1985), over the mid-1980s till 1997–1998, the intermediate target shifted from credit controls toward flexible monetary targeting with "feedback" from inflation and growth. While M3 growth served as a nominal anchor, the operating target was reserve money. The cash reserve ratio (CRR) was the principal operating instrument, along with continued use of some selective credit controls.

But deregulation and liberalization of the financial markets combined with the increasing openness of the economy in the 1990s made money demand more unstable and money supply more endogenous. There were repeated wide deviations from the money supply targets set. The RBI itself noted monetary policy based on demand function of money, as the latter became unstable, could be expected to lack precision (Reddy 2002).

Flexible nominal money supply targeting proved inadequate under these changes, and interest rates were volatile in the 1990s. After the adverse impact of the 1990s' peak in interest rates, the Reserve Bank moved toward an interest rate-based operating procedure, basing its actions on a number of indicators of monetary conditions, including forward-looking expectation surveys (Jalan 2001). It formally adopted a "multiple-indicator approach" in April 1998, following informal changes in practice from the mid-1990s.[3]

There was no formal inflation targeting, but policy statements gave both inflation control and facilitated growth as key objectives. The multiple indicators were the variables affecting future growth and inflation. A specific value of 5 % was given as the desirable rate of inflation, with the aim of bringing it even lower in the long term. Another objective was to reduce reliance on reserve requirements, particularly the CRR, shifting liquidity management toward OMOs in the form of outright purchases/sales of Gsecs and repo and reverse repo operations to affect interest rates. Operating procedures changed as well, with the policy rate becoming the operating instrument and the CMR the operating target. Table 2.1 summarizes these changes. The multiple-indicator approach was criticized as list based. For India, inflation forecast targeting is a natural progression that converts the multiple indicators from an omnibus list to action based on the determinants of inflation, even while retaining vital flexibilities coming from considering a range of information.

---

[3] A vector autoregression model following Christiano et al. (1999) showed the growth of reserve money better indicates the stance of monetary policy for 1985 M1 to 1995 M12 and call money rate for 1996 M1 to 2005 M3. This supports the changing operating procedure of monetary policy in India from quantity to rate variables. The results of forecast error variance decomposition for the later sub period show shocks to exchange rate as major components of unexplained variance of inflation, movements of credit and money supply growth. These findings highlighted the growing importance of the exchange rate channel. While agricultural shocks were the main driving factor of domestic inflation from mid-1980s to mid-1990s, their explanatory power went down substantially post-reform, with international factors becoming the main inflation drivers (Agrawal 2008).

Table 2.1 Monetary policy procedures

Monetary policy	1950s to end 1980s	Early 1990s to 1998–1999	1998–1999 to present
Objectives	(1) Stability	(1) Inflation	(1) Inflation
	(2) Development	(2) Credit supply for growth	(2) Growth
Intermediate target	Priority sector credit targeting	Monetary targeting with annual growth in broad money (M_3) as intermediate target	Multiple-indicator approach (rates, credit, external, fiscal variables, and expectation surveys used for growth and inflation projections)
Operating procedure (instruments)	Direct instruments (interest rate regulations, selective credit control, SLR, CRR)	Gradual interest rate deregulation CMR; direct instruments (selective credit control, SLR, CRR)	Direct (CRR, SLR) and indirect instruments (repo operations under LAF and OMOs)

2.2 Excess Demand or Cost Shocks?

The official understanding of monetary policy in India is that huge monetary overhang built up due to financing of large fiscal deficits created excess demand that had to be sharply reduced during periods of high inflation. But Mohanty (2010) in his Table 1.2 shows that every period of double-digit inflation in India was associated with a supply shock. The relative share of cost shocks and excess demand in Indian inflation is an unsettled question.

Was monetary growth excessive? Chart 2.1 shows growth of reserve money (RM), broad money (M), and real GDP since the 1950s. Chart 2.2 shows WPI inflation. RM shows large fluctuations from the 1970s, demonstrating the limited control left with the RBI. The fluctuations reduce in the 1990s after the removal of automatic monetization. But large inflows push it up again in the 2000s. The fluctuations in broad money are much lower, however, demonstrating greater control through use of the CRR and SLR. The large early fluctuations in output growth and inflation occur during periods of supply shocks, and both moderate from the mid-1990s. '

Table 2.2 helps to further understand these stylized facts and to decide whether growth of money was excessive. Since the table normalizes a measure of monetary

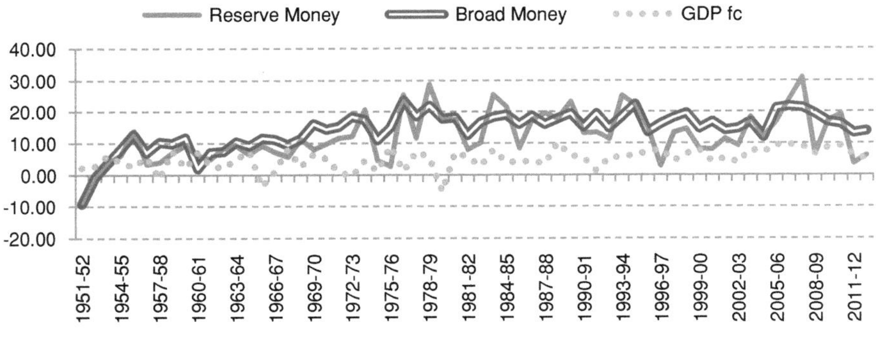

Chart 2.1 Growth rates

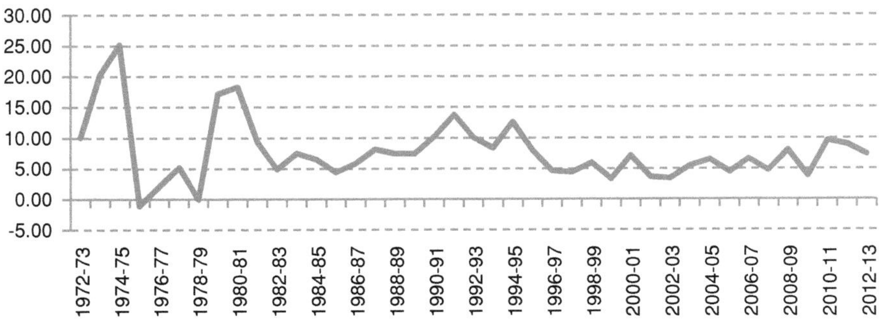

Chart 2.2 Inflation: WPI (AC)

Table 2.2 Policy and outcomes in high inflation and other years

Years	Demand shock	Demand shock without CAD	Monetary policy shock	Fiscal shock	Policy shock	Credit shock	Real GDP growth	WPI inflation
1953–1956	0.5	0.6	0.84	0.59	1.4	0.68	0.2	−2.47
1956–1957	**−1.8**	**0.6**	**−2**	**−0.22**	**−2.22**	**−2.49**	**2.4**	**13.96**
1957–1963	−0.5	−0.6	−0.06	0.6	0.5	0.27	−0.4	3.56
1963–1968	**0.4**	**0.5**	**−0.6**	**0.65**	**0.1**	**−0.37**	**1**	**10.05**
1968–1972	1.8	1.5	0.25	0.06	0.3	−0.03	1.2	3.39
1972–1975	**0.3**	**0.4**	**−0.4**	**−0.4**	**−0.8**	**−0.6**	**1.8**	**18.5**
1975–1979	0.6	0.3	0.7	1	1.8	0.8	5.8	1.6
1979–1981	**−3.7**	**−3.1**	**0.4**	**−0.6**	**−0.3**	**−1.3**	**1**	**17.7**
1981–1990	−0.7	−0.6	0.3	0.4	0.7	0.67	5.4	8
1990–1993	**−1.1**	**−1.3**	**−0.4**	**−0.9**	**−1.3**	**−0.6**	**4**	**11.4**
1993–1994	1.6	0.3	1.3	0.1	1.4	−0.5	5.7	8.4
1994–1995	**1.2**	**1.8**	**0.6**	**−0.6**	**0.1**	**1.8**	**6.4**	**12.6**
1995–2008	0.6	0.66	−0.14	−0.1	−0.3	2.04	7	5.2
2008–2009	**−3.05**	**−2.05**	**0.50**	**1.4**	**1.9**	**2.79**	**6.7**	**8.1 (9.02)**
2009–2010	−0.05	0.46	0.00	0.2	0.2	0.97	8.6	3.8 (12.41)
2010–2013	**−1.78**	**−1.11**	**−1**	**−0.4**	**−1.4**	**0.57**	**6.8**	**8.6 (11.72)**

Note Figure in bold indicates the years in which inflation was in double digits. Figures in brackets in the last column indicate CPI (IW) inflation
CAD current account deficit; *WPI* wholesale price index; *GDP* gross domestic price; *CPI (IW)* consumer price inflation, industrial workers

and fiscal policy by GDP, it is possible to assess whether policy changes were excessive in relation to GDP. Moreover, growth was not excessive over the period as a whole since the negative and positive values largely cancel out. But large negative and positive values in a period imply over-reaction in that period. Policy was not smoothed enough.

The table also captures the monetary and fiscal response to supply shocks added up in the "policy" variable. The bold figures indicate periods of inflation above 8 %. These were all periods of adverse supply shocks. A negative value implies policy contraction exceeding that in GDP. Measuring the policy response to an exogenous shock helps to cut through the endogeneity plaguing macroeconomic systems. Policy reacts to the shocks and affects the outcomes in such episodes.

The fiscal shock is calculated as the rate of change of Central Government revenue, and capital expenditure each as a percentage of GDP. That is, period t gives the total of the three variables each minus their respective values in period t-1. This is then averaged to get per-annum rates. The monetary policy shock is calculated as the change in reserve money growth before 2004 and the change in the policy repo rate after 2004. The table shows policy contraction (negative entries) in most years when the GDP growth rate fell due to a supply shock. Thus, policy amplified shocks since the contractionary impulse exceeded the fall in output.

The "credit" variable does a similar calculation for broad money M3, bank credit to the commercial sector, and total bank credit, capturing outcomes of policy tightening. This was more severe in the earlier shocks. The availability of more financial substitutes and of external finance reduced the impact of policy tightening on credit variables, although its rate of growth fell after the GFC. In the later years, policy was acting more through prices (interest rate changes) than quantities.

Finally, the "demand" variable is the sum of changes in private final consumption expenditure (PFCE), government expenditure (G), Gross Domestic Capital Formation (GDCF), and current account deficit (CAD) as a percentage of GDP. It is also given without the CAD.[4]

Monetary and fiscal policy both tended to be procyclical.[5] The only shock period in which both were countercyclical together was 2008–2009 when the GFC constituted a large negative external demand shock. International pressures and

---

[4] A CAD implies domestic resources are less than domestic requirements and part of domestic demand is leaking abroad since it is met by imports. Including it reduces demand even more as the CAD tends to widen during downswings in India. Goyal (2011b) does a similar analysis for the individual years of external shocks.

[5] Dash and Goyal (2000) found monetary policy broadly succeeded in preventing an explosive growth in money supply and reined in inflationary expectations. But by targeting manufacturing prices it harmed real output. Their estimations implied it would be more efficient to target agricultural prices for inflation control. A monetary contraction should be completed earlier than in the past, and should coincide with a rise in food prices. Information available in the systematic structural features was not exploited in designing monetary policy. Policy would then be countercyclical. Reserve Bank monetary control had intensified shocks to real output, while being unable to prevent the expansion of credit in response to a profit motive.

examples perhaps explain this departure from traditional Indian policy. The stimulus helped a quick recovery, but was sustained too long. The fiscal correction that had started in the early 1990s, after which government expenditures largely grew at or below GDP, was reversed. Monetary policy and fiscal expenditure were also correctly countercyclical over 1995–2008 when demand shocks were positive. They contracted together only in four of the eight high-inflation episodes.

In general, Table 2.2 shows that each shock, plus the policy response, imparted a considerable negative impulse to aggregate demand, even as the supply shock pushed up costs. Demand remained positive through the first oil shock years, but fell steeply in 1979–1981. It was consistently negative through the 1980s, which were the years of largest fiscal deficits and Reserve Bank of India accommodation when the so-called monetary overhang was developed. Since the table measures final demand categories, it maybe large government transfers were siphoned away,[6] perhaps abroad, without reaching beneficiaries to create demand, or they raised prices of inelastically supplied non-traded goods. Rates of inflation and the output sacrifice were lower under recent shocks, although policy reactions remained as severe, suggesting greater resilience and diversity due to a larger share of the private sector.

Although demand shocks remained positive after the mid-1990s, they became highly negative in 2011–2013, as policy contracted too severely to compensate for a too large and extended post-GFC stimulus. Also CPI inflation (in brackets) was much higher than WPI inflation in this period, suggesting bottlenecks in agriculture. Food demand had diversified, but restrictions in agriculture prevented it responding to the changed structure of supply, although there was growth in agricultural productivity.

2.3 Openness, Inflows, and Policy

The other major change with greater openness was the higher level and volatility of foreign inflows. Although capital account convertibility was gradual and sequenced, it still led to large fluctuations in foreign portfolio investment (FPI). The RBI's acquisition of foreign assets was now driving reserve money growth as RBI credit to the government contracted. Reserves of foreign currency accumulated and were sterilized by a contraction of RBI credit to the government partly through OMOs. The latter became possible by the mid-1990s because of the financialliberalization of the previous decade; the debt market was deepening, and government debt could be traded at market-determined rates. The CRR ratios that were being brought down in line with the committee recommendations had to be raised again in a burden-sharing arrangement whereby the costs of sterilization were to be shared by the government, RBI, and banks.

[6] GFI (Global Financial Integrity) (2010) estimated that tax evasion, crime, and corruption removed gross illicit assets from India worth USD 462 billion since independence.

OMOs remained minor for fear of their impact on the cost of government borrowing. Market rates were expected to discipline such borrowing but as real interest rates rose and growth rates fluctuated, government debt burden increased.

Tables 2.3, 2.4 show the changes in India's openness across the decades. Reserves[7] as a ratio of GDP went from a low of 1.35 in the early years to a high of 15.45. Exports plus imports jumped from a stagnant 8–11 % of GDP in the first 40 years after independenceto above 30 %. The dependence on oil imports increased, especially from the 2000s as rising oil prices made oil imports more expensive. The rate of growth of imports was especially high in periods of large oil price shocks. While the current account of the balance of payments remained negative, the capital account jumped to about 3 % of GDP. Exchange rate depreciation was particularly large in the first reform decade. There were sharp depreciations during episodes of sudden capital outflows in the post-GFC period, but they were normally reversed.

Post-reform macrostabilization included a cut in public investment, monetary tightening partly tosterilize capital inflows and an artificial agricultural supply shock as procurement prices for food grains were raised. A benchmark real effective exchange rate was set after two-stage devaluation in the early 1990s, in order to maintain a competitive real exchange rate and encourage exports to aid absorption of excess labor. It was largely maintained. The nominal rate was kept stable for long periods of time, and reserves accumulated under inflows. Growth revived in 1993–1994, and monetary policy was accommodating, but exchange rate volatility in 1995 led to a monetary squeeze that precipitated a slowdown. The monetary stance was relaxed, but reversed again at the first sign of exchange rate volatility. Periodic bursts of volatility, sometimes induced by fluctuations in foreign capital inflows, for example from mid-May to early August 2000, were suppressed. But the sharp jump in interest rates triggered an industrial recession and sustained it over 1997–2001. Goyal (2005) shows in this slowdown period, foreign financial inflows measured as the surplus on the capital account rose, but their volatility fell. The volatility of the CAD, however, rose, suggesting it was policy that was creating volatility in the absorption of inflows. The CAD, which is the difference between investment and domestic savings, is affected by general macroeconomic policy.

Chart 2.3, which graphs components of the BOP as a percentage of GDP, shows the change in reserves to be a mirror image of thecapital account—peak capital flows were largely absorbed in reserves, since they much exceeded the CAD. Chart 2.4 shows the fluctuations in FPI came in through foreign institution investors (FIIs) or their subaccounts registered with the regulator and the steadier increase in foreign direct investment (FDI). Fluctuations in nonresident Indian

[7] FX reserves rose to over 300 billion USD in 2011, compared to a paltry 5 billion in 1990–1991. 30 billion dollars were accumulated in just 18 months over January 2002 to August 2003. Other years of large inflows were 2007 and 2010. Outflows occurred after the global crisis in 2008, were soon reversed, but occurred again whenever global risk aversion rose. Arbitrage occurred at the short end when Indian short real rates were kept higher than US rates.

Table 2.3 External sector indicators (average annual growth rates)

	Reserves	Exports (f.o.b)	Import (c.i.f)	Growth of oil imports	Growth of non-oil imports	Exchange rate depreciation/appreciation
1950–1951 to 1959–1960	−9.13	0.36	7.17	–	–	0
1960–1961 to 1969–1970	10.79	8.87	6.63	–	–	5.15
1970–1971 to 1979–1980	25.26	16.76	20.88	53.47	19.17	0.9
1980–1981 to 1989–1990	1.79	16.62	15.67	12.14	16.45	7.27
1990–1991 to 1999–2000	43.12	19.46	20.01	24.48	17.91	10.66
2000–2001 to 2009–2010	23.36	18.54	20.18	23.57	20.2	1.11
2010–2011 to 2012–2013	8.06	24.97	24.8	31.7	22.98	4.93

Table 2.4 External sector indicators (ratio to GDPmp)

	Reserves	Exports (f.o.b)	Import (c.i.f)	Current account	Capital account	Oil imports	Non-oil imports
1950–1951 to 1959–1960	6.56	5.14	6.79	−0.82	0.28	–	–
1960–1961 to 1969–1970	1.35	3.11	5.01	−1.62	1.57	–	–
1970–1971 to 1979–1980	2.30	3.77	4.61	−0.10	0.59	1.31	4.09
1980–1981 to 1989–1990	2.46	4.02	6.85	−1.44	1.23	2.01	5.15
1990–1991 to 1999–2000	4.75	6.72	9.08	−1.22	1.98	2.11	7.12
2000–2001 to 2009–2010	14.61	10.13	14.32	−0.31	2.82	4.85	11.56
2010–2011 to 2012–2013	15.45	12.95	20.51	−2.84	3.11	7.88	16.92

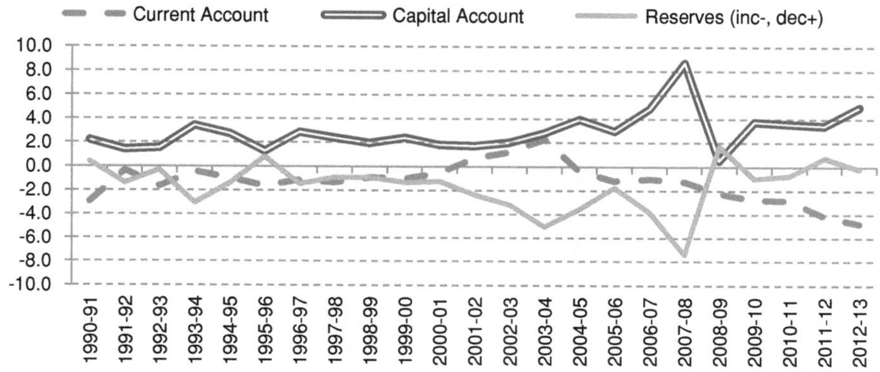

Chart 2.3 India's balance of payments (as a % to GDP)

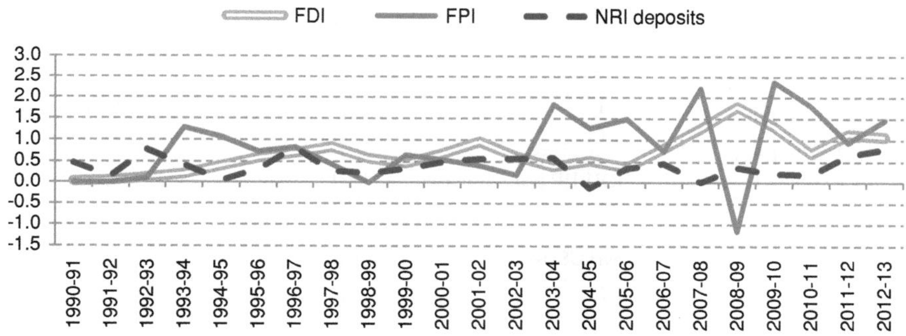

Chart 2.4 Capital inflows to India (as a % to GDP)

deposits reflect interest rate arbitrage limited by shifting policy caps on interest rates.

Overtime capital flows affect international debt or, as it is known in India, the country's International Investment Position (Table 2.5). India's strategic choices in capital account convertibility imply liabilities comprise mostly FDI and foreigner's equity holdings. Assets largely reflect the rise in foreign exchange (FX) reserves, and some outward FDI. The reserves are sufficient to cover short-term outflows particularly since equity outflows would reduce in value during a concerted exit. Even so, the short-term debt component has risen above 40 %, in residual maturity terms, which is unhealthy.

Although the exchange rate was said to be market determined, massive RBI intervention continued in order to absorb foreign portfolio inflows. Trend depreciation was facilitated through the 1990s to cover the inflation differential. There was some appreciation due to the weakening of the dollar from 2002. From 2004, there was mild two-way movement of the nominal exchange rate (Chart 2.5). Foreign exchange reserves accelerated in this period. The nominal exchange rate was now a managed float. There was occasional excess volatility, but a crisis was

Table 2.5 Overall international investment position of India (USD billion)

	Sep 2009	Sep 2010	Sep 2011	Sep 2012	Sep 2013 (PR)
Assets	*375.9*	*406.9*	*434.7*	*441.9*	*436.7*
of which					
Direct investment	76.5	91.5	109.1	115.9	120.1
Reserve assets	281.3	292.9	311.5	294.8	277.2
Liabilities	*482.5*	*611.9*	*659.6*	*713.4*	*736.2*
of which					
Direct investment	159.3	197.8	212.9	229.9	218.1
Portfolio investment	106	163.8	161.5	164.6	171.6
Equity securities	85.1	130.5	128	125.7	124.3
Debt securities	20.9	33.3	33.5	39	47.3
Other investment	217.1	250.4	285.2	318.9	346.5
Trade credits	41.9	56.6	66.7	76.9	89.6
Loans	120.7	134.8	158	164.8	168.7
Currency and deposits	46.7	50.5	52.4	67.2	75.2
Other liabilities	7.9	8.5	8.1	10	13.1

Note PR partially revised
Source Extracted from various RBI IIP press releases, see RBI (2014)

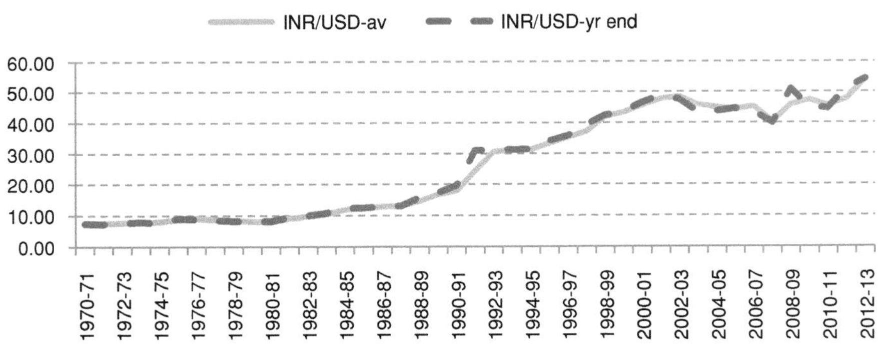

Chart 2.5 Exchange rate

avoided. Even contagion from the East Asian crisis was averted. Over 2003–2007, some agricultural liberalization and falling world food prices did reduce the political pressures that had raised food support prices and inflation. Exchange rate policy was not systematically used to moderate the effect of the typical EM supply shocks: oil price shocks and failure of rains.

Growth rates, moreover, were lower than potential. Monetary tightening in the presence of supply shocks sustained slowdowns. Steady softening of nominal interest rates occurred only after February 2001, as world interest rates fell. A new RBI Governor, Bimal Jalan, demonstrated, through staggered placement of government debt, that it was possible for interest rates to come down despite high fiscal deficits and committed to a soft interest rate regime even while preventing excess volatility of the rupee. There were reversals, however, during periods of exchange rate volatility. In 1998–1999, the decision not to tighten monetary policy when inflation peaked with certain food prices turned out to be correct as inflation fell. Similarly, inflation fell again as the oil shock wore out, without a sharp tightening in monetary policy, both in 2000–2001 and in early 2003–2004.

Sharp defensive rise in interest rates were, however, often implemented given policy makers' perception that interest elasticities continued to be low.[8] Interest rates had been only recently freed; the impact of reforms on elasticities, in particular the impact of the interest rate on consumer spending, was not yet fully understood. In addition, political pressures made the weight given to inflation control high. The RBI had greater autonomy after the reforms, but was not fully independent. The fiscal deficit was thought to be large. There were doubts about the durability of capital inflows and fears of a possible reversal, which would have implied a shock to the risk premium. Finally, risk aversion explained the strong use of the interest rate defense.

Inflation fell in the late 1990s, with improvements in productivity, and the influence of low global inflation in a more open economy, but industrial growth did not revive until 2003, when Indian interest rates followed falling global rates and public expenditure on infrastructure rose. The lowering occurred not from a conscious policy decision but because international interest rates were falling. Even with higher growth and an extended period of high global oil prices, inflation remained low.

2.4 Money Markets and Interest Rates

Throughout this period, gradual financial reforms deepened markets. As most interest rates stopped being administered, the short policy rates became more effective policy instruments. The liquidity adjustment facility (LAF) implemented around that time helped fine-tune domestic liquidity and short-term interest rates drifted downward. The absence of a rate reversal after 2000 contributed to an upswing in activity. Benign market expectations strengthened. Bursts of high volatility in exchange rates were absent during this period. Indian FX markets had

[8] Monetary policy shocks were identified using a short-run vector autoregression model. The identification assumption on contemporaneous causality used to isolate the policy shocks was exogenous shocks (foreign oil price inflation and interest rates), and domestic variables (inflation, IIP growth and exchange rate changes) affect the policy instrument variable (call money rates, or treasury bill rates) contemporaneously, but the policy variables affect them only with a lag. All these variables go on to affect gross bank credit and the broad monetary aggregate (M). Domestic variables do not enter the lag structure of the foreign variables since the Indian economy is too small to affect international prices. The RBI's reaction function or feedback rule to changes in the foreign shocks and non-policy variables determines the setting of the policy instrument variable. The policy shock is the residual from this estimated "reaction" of the RBI. It is orthogonal to the variables in the RBI's feedback rule. The residuals of the 'monetary policy instrument' equation give an estimate of the large monetary policy shocks in this period (Goyal 2008).

Chart 2.6 Bank rate

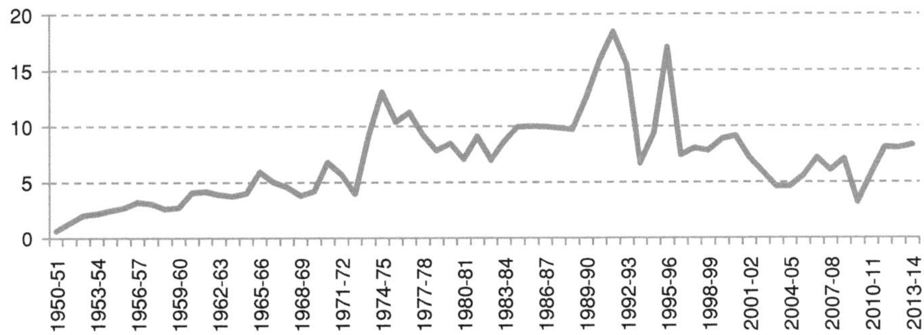

Chart 2.7 Call money rate

the highest growth rates in the world. The fiscal deficit fell after a long time, with higher growth and lower interest rates, when the opposite policy of periodic rise in interest rates had not succeeded in doing this over 1997–2002.

The repo and reverse repo rates began to be changed frequently and smoothly, and the call money rate largely stayed within the band determined by them. Charts 2.6, 2.7, 2.8, 2.9, 2.10, and 2.11 show the changes in the interest rate regime, the increasing sophistication of markets, and market determination of rates. The RBI's general refinance rate, the bank rate, peaked in the early 1990s and fell after that, but was not changed very frequently (Chart 2.6). Volatility in the call money rate (CMR) was much lower after the mid-1990s. Although liberalization initially increased the volatility of rates in a thin market, it eventually brought down volatility, as markets deepened, to levels prevailing when rates were tightly administered. But now, rates came through a complex market process (Chart 2.7).

Chart 2.8 shows the SLR and CRR rates peaking (at, respectively, 37.25 and 14.75) in the early 1990s and then coming down as the repressed financial regime was dismantled. The RBI absorbed liquidity at the reverse repo and injected it at the repo. Charts 2.7 and 2.8 show the bands created by the repo and reverse repo rates as the LAF matured and was actively used after 2004. By this time, most of the sector refinance facilities had been wound up. Chart 2.9 gives the daily

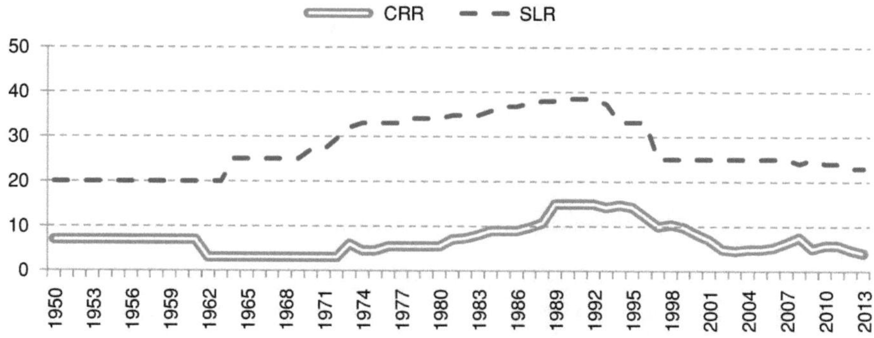

Chart 2.8 Reserve and liquidity ratios: Annual averages

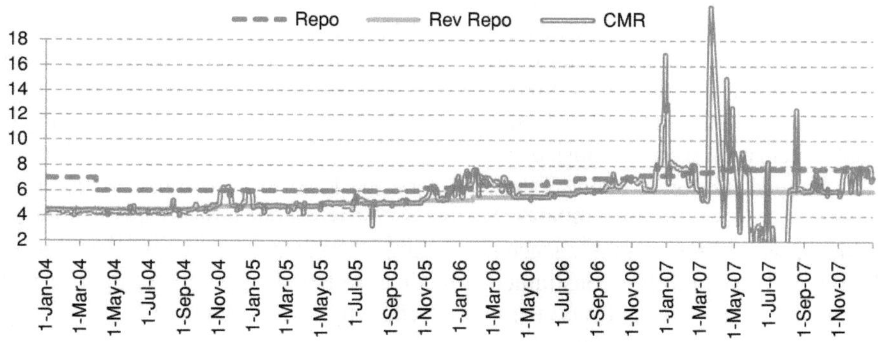

Chart 2.9 Daily policy rates: 2004–2007

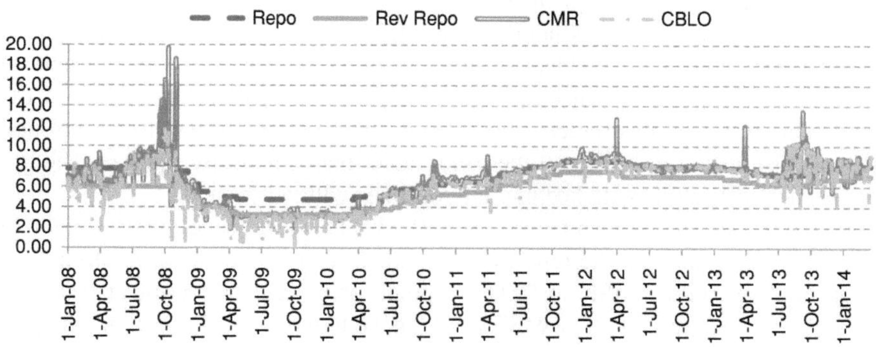

Chart 2.10 Daily policy rates: 2008–2014

CMR. This peaked briefly in 2007 when the RBI limited borrowing in the LAF to encourage the development of the interbank market.

The collateralized borrowing and lending market was developed and rapidly grew to be the largest because of prudential limits on bank borrowing in the call

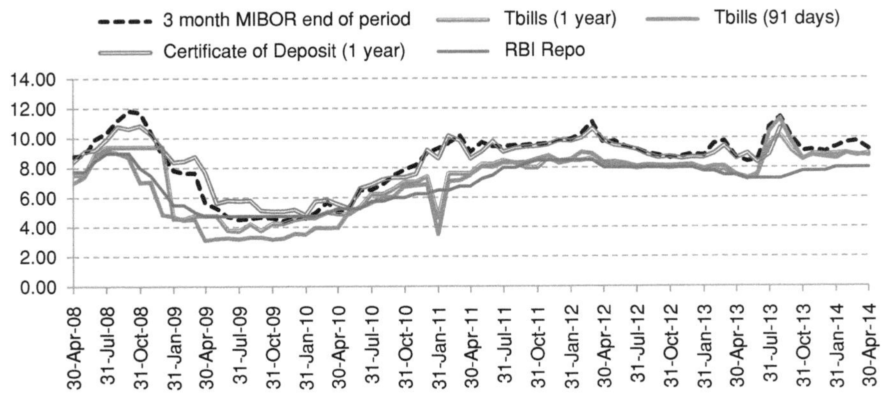

Chart 2.11 Transmission of RBI repo rates

money market. The latter was made a pure interbank market. The CBLO rates are also shown in Chart 2.10. Since lending was based on collateral, market rates could be above the upper band during periods of tight liquidity when collateralizable securities were exhausted as in 2010–2011. But for much of the period, rates hugged the lower band as the RBI used the LAF to absorb excess liquidity generated by large foreign inflows. So the volatility of call money rates, although reduced, was still appreciable since they could jump from one edge of the band to the other. Truly liquidity-constrained banks had to borrow in the overnight or call money market so the CMR was the first to reflect monetary tightening.

Chart 2.11[9] shows how the short policy rates influenced longer maturity rates through the term structure, demonstrating one leg of active monetary transmission through rates. Policy was working now with both price and quantity variables. There were large autonomous changes in liquidity due to forex inflows, variations in government cash balances held with the RBI, and banks' behavior. Continued use of CRR changes also added to jumps in liquidity. The RBI was not able to forecast and fine-tune liquidity sufficiently to keep the CMR in the middle of the band. This was also insufficient appreciation that now policy had to act through the cost of funds or a shifting of the band, rather than a liquidity squeeze. The latter was not compatible with keeping interest rates within the band.

Following the recommendations in RBI (2011), these issues were sought to be addressed by making the repo rate the signal of the policy stance with a marginal standing facility (MSF) at 100 basis points above and absorption at 100 basis points below the repo rate. The MSF would make liquidity available up to one percentage of the SLR. Steps were also taken to improve liquidity forecasting and reduce transaction costs in accessing liquidity from the RBI, so as to allow finer-tuning of liquidity requirements and smoother adjustment of market rates.

Chart 2.12 suggests these were inadequate. This shows the TED spread, the difference between the 3-month US T-bill and the 3-month London Eurodollar Deposit Rate, and the Indian equivalent of the TED spread, the Indian 91 day

[9] This chart was part of the background papers prepared for RBI (2011).

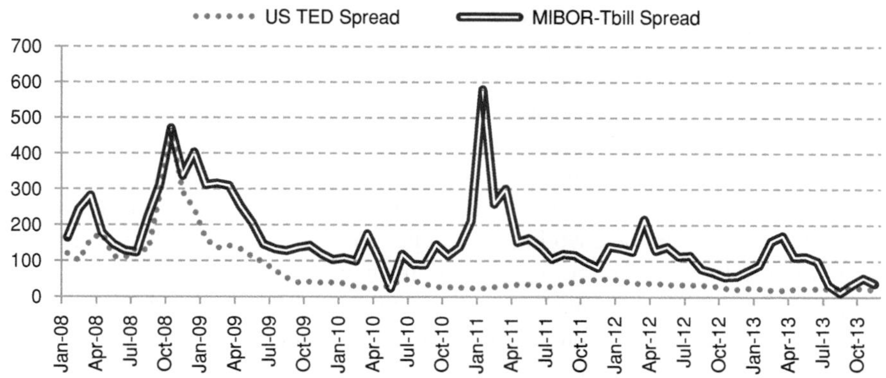

Chart 2.12 The USA and India risk spreads in basis points compared

T-bill yield minus the 3 month Mumbai Interbank offered rate (MIBOR). The difference between the interest rates on interbank loans and on risk-free, short-term government debt (T-bills) is an indicator of rising counterparty risk, or of tightening liquidity in the interbank market. The US TED spread remains generally within the range of 10 and 50 bps (0.1 and 0.5 %), except in times of financial crisis. A rising TED spread often precedes a downturn in the US stock market.

In India, however, these spreads are large even in non-crisis times and peak sharply during periods when markets are squeezed. That they narrowed during the years of large inflows in the mid-2000s suggests that spreads are partly due to tight liquidity or the inability to fine-tune liquidity in response to shocks in government cash balances and in foreign capital flows. If a market is thin, there is such a large impact of a demand or a supply shock.

Curdia and Woodford (2010) argue that, in advanced economies (AEs), a change in spreads has implications for optimal monetary policy. A larger, persistent spread in EMs indicates a requirement for structural reform, but the changes in the spread due to liquidity shocks have to be reduced or compensated for through lower rates, together with vigilant prudential policy to prevent bubbles in thin specific markets. Liquidity tightening and use of the interest ratedefense also have a larger impact on EMs to the extent large spreads raise the average level of lending rates.

RBI moved in 2014 to shift markets to term repo by restricting borrowing in the LAF repo. This should contribute to preventing a widening of TED spreads as the term repo market develops and helps smooth liquidity with less dependence on the RBI (Chart 2.12).

2.5 The Global Crisis, Response, and Revelation of Structure

Inflation rose after the severe international food price and oil shocks over 2007–2008 prompted a steep monetary tightening despite slowing industrial output. The global crisis worsened the crash in industrial output. International credit froze, trade fell, domestic liquidity dried up due to outflows, and fear stalled consumption and investment plans. The global push for concerted macroeconomic stimulus allowed Indian macroeconomic policy, despite high government debt, to be countercyclical for the first time during an external shock. Fiscal stimulus amounted to about 3 % of GDP. RBI made available potential primary liquidity of about 7 % of GDP. Just after the crisis, India was regarded as a high-risk country with low fiscal capacity, but the rapid monetary–fiscal response helped give it a V-shaped recovery with one of the highest world growth rates (6.7 %) during the crisis year with growth rising to 8.6 % the next year. The financial system remained sound. The potential of countercyclical macroeconomic policy was demonstrated.

Shocks hitting the economy can serve as experiments helping to reveal its structure. Consider the summer of 2008. The economy was thought to be overheating after a sustained period of about 9 % growth. International food and oil spikes had contributed to high inflation. The sharp monetary tightening raising short rates above 9 % in the summer of 2008, and the fall of Lehman in September, which froze exports, was a large demand shock. Industrial output fell sharply in the last quarter, but WPI-based inflation only fell with oil prices in the end of the year, and CPI inflation remained high. Demand shocks with a near-vertical supply curve should affect inflation more than output. But the reverse happened. Output growth fell much more than inflation (Table 2.6).

Such outcomes are possible only if inflation is supply determined, but demand determines output. This is the precise sense in which the economy is supply constrained. Components of demand such as consumer-durable spending, housing, etc., are interest sensitive. During the crisis, the lag from policy rates to industry was only 2–3 quarters for a fall and one quarter for a sharp rise. Policy rates have impacted output growth since 1996, while supply constraints affect inflation.[10]

The V-shaped recovery also indicated a reduction in demand rather than a leftward shift of a vertical supply curve. A destruction of capacity would be more intractable; recovery would take longer. Since labor supply ultimately determines potential output for the aggregate economy, the region has a large growth potential.

The crisis response was fast, but the resurgence of inflation before recovery was firmly established led to policy dilemmas regarding exit. The sharp rise of WPI inflation by Q3 of 2009 was regarded as surprising since industry had barely recovered. But it should have been expected given the impact of sustained high CPI inflation on wages. Because of the latter, the manufacturing price index fell only for a few months and had risen to its November 2008 value of 203 by April 2009. Arguments that the economy was overheating were probably incorrect because of the sharp rebound in investment after the four-quarter slump, while growth in private consumption and bank credit remained low. Growth in government consumption also slowed.

But not enough was done to anchor inflationary expectations and to reduce constraints in agricultural markets. A poor monsoonin 2009 and protracted rains

[10] Parts of these arguments have also been made in Goyal (2011b, 2012a).

Table 2.6 Growth, inflation, and policy rates

	2008–2009: Q1–Q4				2009–2010: Q1–Q4				2010–2011: Q1–Q4				2011–2012: Q1–Q4			
	Q1	Q2	Q3	Q4	Q1	Q2	Q3	Q4	Q1	Q2	Q3	Q4	Q1	Q2	Q3	Q4
Growth (Y-o-Y) (%) (constant 2004–2005 prices)																
GDP at factor cost	7.9	7.7	5.8	5.9	6.3	8.6	7.3	9.4	8.5	7.6	8.2	9.2	8.0	6.7	6.1	5.3
Manufacturing	7.0	6.6	2.6	1.3	2.0	6.1	11.4	15.2	9.1	6.1	7.8	7.3	7.3	2.9	0.6	−0.3
GFCF/GDP[a]	33.0	34.8	31.5	32.7	30.4	31.9	30.9	34.5	32.2	34.0	32.3	31.4	33.9	33.4	30.3	30.9
Inflation (Y-o-Y) (%)																
WPI	9.6	12.5	8.6	3.2	0.5	−0.1	5.0	10.2	11.0	9.3	8.9	9.3	9.4	9.7	8.9	7.0
CPI-IW	7.8	9.0	10.2	9.5	8.9	11.6	13.2	15.1	13.6	10.5	9.3	9.0	8.9	9.2	8.4	7.2
Policy rate																
RBI repo	8.0	9.0	7.3	5.3	4.8	4.8	4.8	4.8	5.3	5.8	6.2	6.6	7.2	8.1	8.5	8.5

Source CSO press release and Reserve Bank of India and revised from Goyal (2012a, b)
Note [a]This row is a ratio not a growth rate

in 2010 aggravated food price inflation. Nominal and real wage inflation rose in response. CPI inflation finally began to fall with a bumper harvest in 2011. But then, the Euro debt crisis, global risk-off outflows due to rising risk aversion, and a sharp INR depreciation hit inflation again.

The response to early signs of industrial inflation was delayed, given the very large cut in interest rates that had to be reversed. The delay led to too fast a pace of increase in interest rates[11] and to quantitative tightening. The latter contributed to volatility in interest rates and in industrial output. Table 2.6 again shows industrial output crashing when policy rates peaked over Q3–Q4 2011, while inflation remained high. Monetary policy affected growth much more than inflation.

Government expenditure pumped into the informal sector increased demand for food. Demand for currency actually increased, and financial disintermediation occurred in response to inflation. Financing for firms was coming from abroad as domestic credit growth remained slow. Firming oil prices added to wage pressures from food inflation, and costs rose. Liquidity remained tight, and demand contracted. Growth in industrial production softened and that in investment also fell sharply in Q1 of 2011.

The events bring out frequent supply shocks and also show a large impact of demand on output, and of supply shocks on inflation, suggesting the AD AS analysis of Sect. 1.3.4 is applicable. It becomes more so as higher growth paths became well established during catchup growth. The longer-run aggregate supply is elastic given youthful populations in transition to more productive occupations, but it is subject to frequent negative supply shocks (Fig. 1.1).

If policy is better based on this structure and shocks, it could more successfully smooth cycles and maintain growth. With a primary food or oil price supply shock, the aggregate supply curve in the figure shifts upward and propagation mechanisms sustain higher inflation. If in response, a demand contraction shifts the aggregate demand curve downward, this reduces inflation only marginally and at a high cost in terms of output lost. Policy should instead restrict demand just sufficiently to prevent inflationary wage and price expectations shifting up the supply curve through second round effects, while encouraging supply-side improvements that can shift down the AS curve. As elasticities increase and systems become more complex, blunt instruments can be phased out and policies designed to reduce sharp changes. The relative elasticities of AS and AD curves suggest that although pricing power of firms does rise when demand is high, they tend to pass on cost shocks even if demand is low because of the rise in intramarginal costs. Fixed costs can be absorbed more easily when output is growing.

It is difficult to come across unemployment estimates, but numbers unemployed are large. In the developed countries, output was regarded as below potential because the crisis left 22 million unemployed. In India, the over 300 million below the poverty line are not meaningfully employed. Given the youthful

[11] The operative rate went from the reverse repo at 3.25 in March 2010 to the repo at 8.5 by October 2011.

demographic profile, 10–12 million are expected to enter the labor force every year. The Planning Commission estimates it will take growth at 10 % per annum together with an employment elasticity of 0.25 to absorb them. Since peak levels of domestic savings plus inflows had reached 40 % of GPD, with an incremental capital output ratio of 4, this gives 10 % rate of growth. This could be regarded as the potential output. The RBI, however, defines full capacity as the potential output of the manufacturing sector, even though in India, for example, this accounts for only 20 % of the output and 5 % of the employment. The economy is considered to be supply constrained.

Figure 1.1 helps understand how exactly the economy is supply constrained and better captures the macroeconomic structure of an economy in transition. The economy is supply constrained in the sense inefficiencies on the supply-side perpetuate inflation although output is largely demand determined. Demand contractions amplify shocks, but are not major independent sources of shocks. Goyal and Arora (2013) argue, in such circumstances, the economy should be regarded as having reached potential growth if second round pass-through is causing supply shocks to plateau above a threshold level. They find, however, that the post-GFC period was characterized by multiple supply shocks rather than sustained propagation.

Political and institutional features also result in fiscal–monetary combinations such that the economy remains on an elastic stretch of the aggregate supply curve. Fiscal populism pushes monetary authorities toward conservatism in order to reduce inflationary expectations. But since populism raises inefficiencies and therefore costs, it shifts up the supply curve, while monetary tightening reduces demand, resulting in a large negative effect on output for little reduction in inflation. For the RBI to be accommodating, restraint on revenue deficits and wasteful expenditure is necessary.

2.5.1 Post-Crisis CAD and Exchange Rates

After the GFC, there were many external shocks[12] from commodity prices and fluctuations in foreign capital flows. Inelastic oil and inflation-driven demand for gold contributed to a widening of the CAD, and its financing became an issue. But capital flows fluctuated following global risk-on–risk-off cycles unrelated to domestic needs and drove sharp changes in the exchange rate. Just talk of quantitative easing (QE) withdrawal (known as the taper on) led to steep depreciation and loss of EM asset values in May 2013. By March 2014, sentiment had reversed. But a surge of capital normally ends in a sudden stop. The worst case for India, of oil shocks and global risk-off occurring together, happened in late 2011 with the Euro debt crisis.

[12] This section draws on material from Goyal (2014a).

2.5.1.1 Causes of CAD Widening

The CAD (Chart 2.3) was relatively stable in the post-reform period, varying between −3 and +2.3 as a ratio of GDP, until after the GFC when it first fell below −3, regarded as the sustainable limit. It even reached -6.5 % in Q3 2012–2013.

Post-GFC increments in reserves were small since inflows about equaled the CAD. But in Q3 2011–2012, inflows fell far short of the CAD. Despite some sale of reserves, the rupee slumped to 55.[13] Inflows revived somewhat in Q4, and the rupee came back toward 50. Many macrovariables adjust to achieve the balance of payments (BOP) tautology that the capital plus the current account must equal the change in reserves. So widening the CAD may not have been responsible for the depreciation of the INR. The post-GFC suggests the following:

1. Although India required a higher level of inflows to finance a widening CAD, it was the fall in inflows, not the CAD, that was primarily responsible for rupee depreciation. When inflows were plentiful, CADs were financed without depreciation.
2. External risk-off caused outflows more than the CAD. Major risk-off periods when there were outflows from most EMs back to AE safe havens included the European debt crisis, the US taper-on announcement, and January 2014 due to problems in Argentina and Turkey.
3. So the CAD itself was partly due to external shocks, even as global risk-off aggravated financing issues. But during risk-off periods, countries with higher CADs did experience more outflows. And depreciation itself worsened the CAD.

That there were twin deficits, a FD as well as a CAD, points to generalized excess demand that policy could have contained. However, even as the CAD widened in 2011–2012, India's GDP growth rate fell to 6.5 %, compared to 8.4 % in the previous year. Further widening of the CAD in the next year accompanied even lower growth of 5 %. Growth in aggregate demand categories like consumption and fixed investment also fell. Table 2.2 shows a large negative demand shock over 2010–2013. As against this, the CAD was only 1.3 % in 2007–2008, a year of high consumption and investment when output grew at above 9 %. So supply shocks rather than excess demand widened the CAD.

Analysis of cycles also supports the supply shocks explanation. The trade surplus (net exports, NX) is procyclical in India rather than countercyclical as it would be if it was driven by domestic demand. Correlation of NX normalized by output and output (NX/Y with Y) is positive. NX/Y tends to fall in periods of low growth, associated with low external demand, rather than falling when rising growth and domestic demand raise imports (Goyal 2011b).

[13] For the year as a whole the CAD was 4.2 % compared to capital inflows at 3.7 %. The RBI's draw-down of reserves, amounting to 12.8 billion USD, made up the difference. In 2012–2013 the CAD peaked at 4.8 %, before coming down the next year.

Such an inverse relationship between the CAD and growth can occur if as exports rise they raise growth and NX. On the other hand, a sudden collapse of export markets, due to a global shock, reduces growth and decreases NX. If oil shocks raise costs, and set in a contraction, NX would again fall along with falling growth as imports rise. The period after the financial crisis saw both a collapse in export markets and a rapid resumption in oil price hikes. These external shocks drove the trade deficit.

As incomes fall (especially as firm profits and government revenues fall), so do savings. The CAD must equal I–S by definition. Investment falls in slowdowns, but if savings fall even more, the CAD widens. Financial savings finance investment that requires traded goods imports, while physical savings, such as in real estate, are invested more in non-traded goods. So a fall in financial savings widens the trade and current account deficits more. Financial disintermediation due to the absence of inflation hedges raises the demand for gold, thus reducing financial savings as well as directly increasing imports.

The FD widened due to the coordinated global stimulus pushed by the G-20. The fiscal stimulus was kept in place too long because of the uncertain global recovery. As the Government, concerned about rating downgrades, made a serious effort to reduce the FD in the last quarter of 2012, fall in government consumption reduced growth in services but not the CAD, suggesting government expenditure largely created demand for non-tradable goods, and for a varied food basket. Excess demand was a problem only in agriculture, where supply rigidities prevent expansion to keep up with demand for food variety (Goyal 2012b), while a depreciating INR prevented imports from offering a low-cost solution.

2.5.1.2 Policy Errors

Even if supply shocks, and the consequent expensive imports, and higher inflation were largely responsible for the widening CAD, there was aggravation from policy mistakes. Domestic supply bottlenecks raised coal imports, just as a faltering world demand reduced export growth. The administered pricing regime reduced substitution away from expensive oil imports. A paucity of inflation protected savings instruments reduced financial savings and increased the demand for gold. No action was taken on constraints in agricultural marketing that boosted food inflation.

Although crude oil dominates the import basket, a structural rise in imports does occur with higher growth. Ultimately, exports have to rise to finance these. Policy that relies on depreciation to stimulate exports, without building export capacity and lowering costs, is inadequate. For example, India's per-container trade costs were more than twice the East Asia's average. Bureaucratic delays and hurdles prevented it becoming part of Asian export supply chains.

Caps on foreign investment in government debt had been raised to USD 30 billion in 2013 (overall limit 81 billion including corporate bonds). Negative debt flows occurred after Bernanke's May 2013 taper-on statement because of an expected strengthening of US bond yields. Indian market positions were largely long in government debt as interest rates were in a downward phase. But yields rose with the policy response to debt outflows that raised short rates by 300 basis points (Table 2.7). There were large domestic market losses as bond values fell.

But even in September 2013, the share of debt securities at 36 % of equity securities and 6 % of total liabilities was still small. So unnecessary policy tightening, not debt outflows, drove the rise in yields in the Indian context.[14] Policy did not utilize degrees of freedom from the careful sequencing of capital account convertibility. Research at the IMF (2014) showing bond mutual funds, especially retail funds, which are twice as sensitive as equity mutual funds to global sentiment, underlines the wisdom of the sequencing.[15]

The other policy mistake was in not taking adequate steps to reverse the exit of domestic households from capital markets. As a result, FPI-driven volatility dominated domestic markets. Volatility could have been reduced by raising the share of household financial savings by offering more instruments suiting household needs, and by liberalizing market participation of domestic pension funds.

The rising debt and share of FIs played a role in convincing authorities that markets were too large and reserves too small for the RBI to intervene. But this was not true since reserves were still large compared to the volatile component of foreign liabilities, debt, and equity securities (Table 2.5). Indian reserves satisfied various criteria of reserve adequacy used such as comparing them to the sum of short-term external debt plus CAD, or CAD minus FDI inflows. Leaving the rupee wholly to markets over 2009–2011 without preemptive action against sharp depreciations was therefore another major policy mistake.

2.5.1.3 Managing the Exchange Rate

EMs face capital flows that respond to global, not to domestic conditions, thin markets, and more volatile risk premiums. All these aggravate the tendency for exchange rates to overshoot fundamental values, so the value of the currency cannot be left to markets alone. The post-GFC capital flows in response to external events created perverse movements in the exchange rate showing a full float is not yet viable. The academic literature also has shifted away from advocating corner regimes of a full float or tight fix for EMs toward middling regimes. China managed successful catchupgrowth with a fixed nominal exchange rate. India chose to develop markets earlier because of its advantage in financial services, so it has to

[14] Debt outflows over May 22–August 26th were 868 USD million for Indonesia, where foreign funding of domestic currency sovereign bonds had been liberalized considerably, compared to 35 USD million for India. So Indonesia had to raise policy rates 175 basis posts post taper-on. IMF (2013) in a regression of domestic on US yields finds a significant coefficient (1.1) for Indonesia compared to insignificant (−0.3) for India.

[15] In a sensible application of this logic, the RBI in 2014 disallowed FPI investments in Gsecs of less than one year maturity, in anticipation of possible future taper-related volatility.

Table 2.7 The policy measures taken over 2010–2013

Date	Change in INR/USD (week before)	Change in INR/USD (week after)	Policy action
December 28, 2010	−0.21	0.03	RBI issues guidelines for OTC FX derivatives and overseas hedging
February 1, 2011	0.11	−0.48	Derivatives guidelines applied
September 15, 2011	1.82	1.83	Exchange earners foreign currency account and residents foreign currency accounts liberalization
November 15, 2011	1.19	1.54	Increase in ceiling rate on banks' export credit in foreign currency by 150 basis points
December 5, 2011	−0.77	2.18	Speech reinforcing RBI's hands-off policy
December 15, 2011	2.79	−1.51	Bank net open position limits (NOPL) reduced 75 %; free cancellation and rebooking of FX forward contracts disallowed
May 21, 2012	1.04	0.90	Netting of positions in currency futures/options with OTC positions disallowed; position limits of banks for currency futures and options reduced
September 11, 2012	0.07	−1.18	ECB policy eased
May 13, 2013	0.96	0.12	RBI restricts banks' gold imports
May 22, 2013	0.89	0.58	Bernanke says Fed may taper QE
June 20, 2013	1.43	−0.001	Foreign banks open positions in USD/INR reduced to almost zero
July 9, 2013	0.93	−0.71	Any proprietary activity by banks in currency futures banned
July 10, 2013	0.72	−0.42	Public sector oil companies directed to buy FX only from one bank (SBI)
July 23, 2013	−0.36	1.43	Monetary tightening measures started from July 9; reduced LAF limit to 0.5 % of a bank's own NDTL; banks to maintain a daily minimum CRR balance of 99 %; MSF rate raised to 10.25, and CMR moved up to it from repo of 7.25
August 28, 2013	4.63	−2.32	FX swap window for oil companies (closed end November)
September 4, 2013	1.36	−3.24	Window for the banks to swap the fresh FCNR(B) deposits with RBI and increase in Banks' overseas borrowing limit with option of swap with RBI
September 18, 2013	−1.07	−0.92	Fed refrains from QE taper, keeps bond buying at USD 85 billion
November 11, 2013	1.89	−0.74	Participation by SEBI registered FIIs, QFI long-term investors in credit enhanced bonds

allow a more flexible market-determined exchange rate. The float, however, has to be managed as argued in Sect. 1.3.4.

In the absence of management, does a sharp depreciation help exports? Or should policy try to maintain an undervalued real exchange rate? A fall in export growth and a widening CAD accompanied depreciation from INR/USD 45 in early 2011 to 67 in September 2013, when depreciation is supposed to improve both CAD and exports. While depreciation corrects for inflation differentials, it itself contributes to inflation, as imports and import substitutes become costly, leading to a vicious cycle of higher inflation requiring more depreciation. Repeated bouts of sharp depreciation contributed to sticky Indian inflation and hardened inflation expectations. Post-2011 growth fell, while inflation remained high and sticky. A sharp depreciation and high volatility also does not help exporters, especially since appreciation followed the depreciation as inflows returned. Pass-through to import prices of commodities is faster, while that to exports is incomplete and delayed.

The global cycle also matters. In a period of low global demand, depreciation cannot increase exports but adds to import costs. In EMs, sustained depreciation tends to raise country risk leading not to expected appreciation back toward fundamentals but to fears of further weakening. So taking a sharp INR depreciation need not even facilitate lower interest rates from uncovered interest parity (UIP) (see footnote 17).

Over the longer term, an undervalued real exchange rate does increase exports, as the Chinese experience demonstrates. But to be sustained, it requires a disciplined labor market, where real wages do not rise. Chinese wages rose after many years of high growth, but Indian wages began to rise much earlier in their catchup cycle. The rise in real wages India experienced over 2007–2013 years requires real appreciation, which will occur through inflation if there is nominal depreciation. Inflation intensified after the sharp 2011 depreciation that reversed earlier real appreciation, since wages continued to rise. For India, a steady competitive REER may be feasible, not an undervalued one. Such a REER may be adequate to maintain healthy export growth, with complementary supply-side measures. The only years of mild real appreciation were 2010–2011 and 2011–2012 which, therefore, cannot be blamed for the export slowdown and CAD widening. In October 2013, the INR recovered to 62, and exports began to grow as global growth revived.

But unfortunately, just in the post-GFC period, although the stated position remained the RBI would act to prevent excess volatility, policy became increasingly hands off. Markets were allowed to determine INR level and volatility subject to what remained of capital controls that continued to be reduced. Intervention was temporarily suspended in 2007 at a time of strong inflows that made sterilization difficult, but resumed to accumulate inflows from October as the market stabilization bonds were negotiated for cost sharing with the government. The INR had to depreciate during post-Lehman equity outflows in order for them to take a write-down in asset values and share risk even as the RBI sold some reserves. Inflows resumed quickly, however, and up to end 2011 were just adequate to finance the CAD (Chart 2.3). So there was hardly any intervention in this period.

This led to the market misperception that the RBI was unable to intervene in FX markets, aided by statements from the RBI about the large size of India's FX liabilities and potential capital movements relative to reserves. As a result, the rupee went into a free fall in end 2011. An environment of low growth and a rising CAD added to the fragility of FX markets.

The RBI did begin to sell reserves in November 2011 as the INR spiraled downward. It also restricted FX markets. Retrospective taxation in budget 2012, and the Fed's taper announcement in May 2013, also led to outflows requiring RBI action.[16] Some of many feasible policy actions, including administrative measures such as controls, market restrictions, intervention or buying and selling in FX markets, signaling, and monetary policy measures such as the classic interest ratedefense, were used, and it is possible to assess their effectiveness.

Table 2.7, which lists the policy measures taken over 2010–2013, attempts this by estimating their impact on the exchange rate; that is, did a measure reverse or add to existing market movements? The table gives the basis points change in the INR/USD rate in the week before and the week after a measure. A negative entry implies an appreciation of the INR and a positive entry the reverse.

The table suggests the most effective measure was the FX swap window announced for oil-marketing companies in end August 2013. Not only did the INR strengthen substantially, but it reversed an existing depreciation, and the rupee continued to gain after that, as other measures were added to the swap window that remained open till end November. Measures that made more FX available, such as the swap window and subsidy for bank foreign borrowing or easier ECB, also appreciated the INR; restrictions on markets such as reducing position limits worked only sometimes. The use of the interest ratedefense in July 2013 was a total failure. Signals that the RBI was unable to intervene and the INR should be left to the markets had a large impact but were also counterproductive. Well-designed signals could, therefore, have the desired effect. Global shocks such as Fed announcements also impacted the INR.

The lessons from this experience are the importance of designing policy in line with the current state of capital account convertibilityand evolution of markets. Given India's growth prospects and relatively greater reliance on growth-driven equity flows, the use of the interest rate defense for the exchange rate was counterproductive and should be avoided at the current juncture, even as restraints continue on debt flows. Equity investors' assets loose value with a sharp depreciation, but an ineffective interest rate defense does not help existing equity investors, even as reduced growth harms new entrants.

The interest rate works by raising the return to holding domestic currency over that to holding international currencies. If expected depreciation is large, the

[16] After zero intervention from January, monthly net purchases in USD million were 10678 over 2007:10 to 2008:10. This switched to net sales of 1505 over 2008:11 to 2009:4 as outflows intensified under the GFC. Average intervention was near zero at monthly net purchases of 285 over 2009:05 to 2011:10. But 2011:10 to 2013:07 saw heavy monthly net sales of 8580.

required rise in short-term interest rates can be very high.[17] To effectively impact the cost of domestic borrowing for speculation, the increase in short-term interest rates also has to be large. The July 300 basis point rise was not large enough to cover expected depreciation yet raised both Indian short- and long-interest rates and intensified the industrial slump. Although Indian interest rates were much higher than the USA's, this could not prevent debt outflows since these tend to be driven by global factors. To the extent capital mobility is not perfect and there is some exchange rate flexibility, the impossible trinity does not hold—there is some freedom in setting policy rates, and these should target the domestic cycle, not the exchange rate.

So in the current stage of capital account convertibility, where interest-sensitive inflows are still a small share of total inflows, it is better if the exchange rate does not directly enter the policy reaction function. The policy rate should respond to the indirect effect of the exchange rate on inflation. Intervention, smoothing net demand, and signaling can all be used to reverse deviations of the exchange ratefrom equilibrium, or prevent excessive depreciation, thus reducing the pressure to raise interest rates.

The RBI's stated position of preventing current and future excess volatility is the correct one, but it needs to be more actively implemented, with an informal 10 % medium-term band for exchange rate movements as discussed in the ideas Sect. (1.3.4). Since under large outflows, the CB comes in after markets bottom out, to make portfolio investors share currency risk, the band may occasionally be breached but should soon revert.

Under adverse expectation-driven outflows, the market demand and supply for FX will not determine an exchange rate based on fundamentals. Smoothing lumpy foreign currency demand in a thin and fragile FX market is useful. Direct provision of FX to oil-marketing companies was first used in the mid-1990s.[18] It is a good way of providing FX reserves to a fragile market without supporting departing capital flows. So there are innovative ways of using reserves, which can be built up again during periods of excessive inflows. Although swaps add exchange rate risk to the RBI's balance sheet, it need not materialize over the short life of the swap if markets are successfully calmed. They also encourage domestic entities to hedge. It is only if these polices are not used effectively that restricting markets may become necessary,[19] despite adverse side effects.

[17] The basic underlying principle is that of UIP, which equalizes the expected returns to holding assets such as bonds in any currency. Since currencies can easily depreciate by 10–40 % in a crisis, short-term interest rates have to rise by as much. On 28th January 2014, even as the policy repo rate was hiked by 25 basis points there were outflows, mostly debt, due to global risk-off from the crash of Argentina's currency and fears of Chinese credit overstretch.

[18] I thank Dr. Y. V. Reddy for this point.

[19] Thus in December 2011, the INR remained under pressure despite a reduction in global risk-on due to ECB announcement of support to bank lending and money market activity (see http://www.ecb.europa.eu/press/pr/date/2011/html/pr111208_1.en.html) due to the RBI's then hands-off policy and reluctance to use reserves, thus necessitating severe market restrictions on December 15th. These brought the INR back from 55 to 50. Adverse tax measures for MNCs in the March 2012 budget triggered outflows and the INR again reached 55, leading to further market restrictions in May 2012.

Various market-restrictive measures reduced market turnover sharply in the currency derivative markets in exchanges, while total turnover including the dominant over-the-counter (OTC) FX trading in banks also fell (Goyal 2014a). This suggests the two types of markets are complements rather than substitutes. Exchanges are thought to be dominated by short-term position taking since no real underlying is required unlike in the RBI-regulated OTC markets. But in FX markets, worldwide portfolio-rebalancing types of transactions between market makers are normally much larger than those based on real exposures. These allow banks as well as small firms that may not get a good deal at banks to lay off risks in futures markets. But expectations are especially important in such markets and can lead to one-way positions.

Under freer capital flows, restricting domestic markets encourages transactions to migrate abroad. Although difficult to measure precisely, the non-deliverable forward (NDF) market may be above 50 % of the onshore market[20] in 2014. It had risen in the period of market restrictions. This is against the objective of developing and deepening domestic markets. Moreover, domestic regulators are unable to influence offshore markets. Therefore, it is better if policy reduces incentives for risk taking in markets rather than forbids transactions.[21] Actions appropriate to the Indian context and reform path were the most effective. Following such a restraint also reduces regulatory discretion that in a complex environment can lead to over- or underkill.

The Global FinancialArchitecture (GFA) is supposed to smooth turbulence and help countries deal with it. But international financial crises have occurred with unfailing regularity. While they normally were restricted to EMs, the GFC originated in AEs.

2.5.1.4 Emerging Markets and the Global Financial Architecture

India's opening out unfortunately happened at a time of many international crises. The GFA, supposed to ensure international financial stability, was shown to be inadequate and in need of reforms. Even as Indian policy makers were responding to external shocks, they had to play a more active role in the GFA. The G-20 was a new institution created after the GFC, due to the recognition that better coordination was required in a more interconnected globe. Although the G-20 lacked the comprehensive legal charter required for a formal international institution, it

[20] There are indications offshore markets rise with restrictions on domestic markets. According to BIS data net turnover from reporting dealers abroad rose from 5.4 USD billion to 6.1, while that from reporting local dealers rose from 11.5 to 12.5 over the 3 years. OTC FX turnover outside the country rose from 50 (20.8 USD billion) to 59 % (36.3 USD billion) of the total (Goyal 2014b).

[21] International, FX markets survived the GFC relatively well partly since boards imposed limits on capital available to traders and they had some liability for losses.

gave a voice to major EMs in global dialogue, potentially reducing the dominance of G-7 countries. It did produce comprehensive reform lists. EMs also got greater representation in some of the international institutions that comprise the GFA, such as the Bank of International Settlement (BIS), and the Financial StabilityBoard (FSB). But the governance structures of the International Monetary Fund (IMF) and World Bank (WB)—which monitor the policies decided on in the G-20—did not change. For example, representation in the IMF's executive board remains incommensurate with EMs growing economic power. Quotas, votes, and voice of EMs all have to change suitably. Insufficient diversity encourages the "groupthink" that the Independent Evaluation Office of the IMF identified as a cause of the lack of action against financial risks that built up before the GFC.

But EMs also did not use their new voice effectively. For example, they brought in a development agenda into the G-20, thus diffusing the required focus on financial reforms. The G-7 perspective continued to dominate and so financial risks continue to build up and the GFA remains fragile. The financial reforms proposed were flawed because of an excessive focus on building capital buffers in banks. Leverage caps have been imposed but are too lax, still allowing bank balance sheets to multiply up to 33 times their equity.

These proposals do not suit EMs, whose financial sectors tend to be bank dominated, but more closely supervised, with broad-pattern regulation that directly reduces leverage. This has better incentive properties, while also reducing regulatory discretion (Goyal 2014b). Bank-based reforms may drive transactions into shadow banks to escape regulation. Since it was difficult to build up capital buffers when banks were weak, these were also delayed. Moreover, buffers have more of a loss-absorbing or shock-insulating rather than a risk-mitigating effect. Reform alternatives such as transaction-based prudential requirements including margins, low taxes, and position limits have the advantage of being naturally countercyclical and reduce excessive risk taking. But they need to be universally adopted in order to prevent arbitrage in favor of a lenient jurisdiction or excluded asset.

Endogenous expansion of leverage, with QE adding to it, was responsible for fluctuations in capital flows to EMs. The search for yield drove up asset prices, including commodity prices, which also impacted EMs even as financial risks built up again. AEs deliberately pumped up global asset prices to help their recovery, ignoring globalspillovers from these actions.

The debate over currency adjustments in the G-20 also illustrates how short-term AE interests were able to prevail, against their own long-term interests and the global recovery. In the 2012 G-20 meeting, finance ministers agreed not to manipulate exchange rates for competitive advantage in the post-GFC slowdown. But interest rate- or liquidity-boosting policy in response to domestic needs, which AEs typically use, and which also affects exchange rates, was not to be regarded as manipulation. In fairness, measures such as intervention and controls that EMs with less developed markets are forced to use should also not be regarded as manipulation. But the premise that all intervention is manipulation and all controls are market distorting tends to force EMs to follow exchange rate regimes appropriate to AEs although EMs may not yet be ready for them.

AEs also use other types of policies to affect exchange rates. For example, Mr. Abe's campaign promise to aid export-dependent manufacturers by bringing down the value of the yen became self-fulfilling since traders acting in advance of expected action depreciated the yen 15 % against the dollar after November 2012. It is a stretch to fit these in interest rate- or liquidity-boosting policy, but G-20 interpreted it as a response to domestic needs. It follows domestic needs of EMs should also be recognized.

The AEs tend to take a view that whatever is good for AEs growth will eventually be good for EMs. That is true, but even so action should be taken to moderate costs imposed on EMs, since slower EM growth in turn reduces recovery in AEs. What is good for EMs can also be good for AEs. AEs are answerable largely to their domestic constituencies—the Fed stimulus did help the USA make the best post-crisis recovery. But the G-20 and the IMF now have ways to pressurize AEs on external spillovers.

In 2012, the IMF introduced Financial Sector Assessment Programmes for all systemically important countries. A new Integrated Surveillance Decision aims to make surveillance more effective. Member countries' obligations under the IMF's Articles of Agreement cannot be changed, but it does enhance the existing legal framework by making Article IV consultations a vehicle for multilateral as well as bilateral surveillance, to also cover spillovers from member countries' policies that may impact global stability. Even without legal commitments, this can bring peer pressure to bear on countries whose imbalances create spillovers on others. A Pilot External Sector Report assesses, in addition to exchange rates,current accounts, balance sheet positions, reserves adequacy, capital flows, and capital account policies.

It seeks to go beyond cyclical factors to identify the impact of policy distortions and other structural and country-specific factors on a country's current account. It asks whether the home country's policies need to change or whether other economies should change course.[22] A IMF staff discussion paper takes the position that while a country can give greater weight to domestic concerns over international spillovers, where the latter impose costs on other countries, there is a case for multilateral coordination that can either ask for a reduction in capital controls or ask lenders to partially internalize the risks of volatile capital flows (Ostry et al. 2012). But it admits the latter is "much thornier"!

It will be a major step toward symmetry if the onus for capital flow volatility is put on source countries also instead of the current system where the entire burden of adjustment is borne by recipient countries. But for adjustment to actually be symmetric, deeper changes moderating asymmetric power in the GFA are required. After the East Asian crisis, EMs reformed, but AEs did not. Nor was the GFA modified. AEs take the position that asset bubbles are not due to QE but due to EM demand, again putting all the onus on EMs. While EMs, including China, are allowing currency appreciation and stimulating domestic demand to correct global imbalances, deficit reduction in AEs has been indefinitely postponed. India allowed its currency to appreciate over 2009–2011 despite a large CAD.

[22] See http://www.imf.org/external/pubs/ft/survey/so/2012/POL071912A.htm.

In return, AEs committed in the 2010 Toronto G-20 meet to "at least halve deficits by 2013 and stabilize or reduce government debt-to-GDP ratios by 2016." But at the 2012 summit in Mexico City, it was admitted this target would not be achieved. Moreover, it was said to be not advisable to reduce deficits given continued global uncertainties. Instead, AEs only committed to "ensure that the pace of fiscal consolidation is appropriate to support the recovery" (Thomson 2012). The argument that in a balance sheet recession when the private sector is deleveraging, and there is a possibility of a debt deflation trap, the government must spend has some validity. Reducing debt and deficits is easier when growth is higher. But if feasible future growth is overestimated, the stimulus given today can be excessive and recreate conditions that led to the GFC. At the very least simple uniform types of financial regulation to moderate spillovers from AE policies in the shape of risky capital flows and commodity price bubbles could be adopted.

AEs pumped up global asset prices to help their recovery, ignoring global spillovers from these actions. The stimulus the Fed undertook did help the USA make the best post-crisis recovery and AEs are answerable largely to their domestic constituencies. But the G-20 and the IMF now have ways to pressurize them on external spillovers. It was hoped, after the May 2013 turbulence, the US taper on would be more sensitive to EM concerns. Taper on is being more carefully designed, with a focus on keeping interest rate expectations well anchored. The reduction of USD 10 billion in December did not affect markets. But in January 2014, the reduction occurred despite trouble in Argentina and Turkey and enhanced these troubles. There were calls for greater global policy coordination, to which the Indian RBI governor rightly contributed. EMs can push for measures that reduce capital flow volatility.

But the ultimate defense against global volatility is in reducing vulnerability to outflows through deepening domestic markets and other structural reforms, even as in the short term a reduced CAD and larger reserves reduce the skittishness of capital flows. In the absence of meaningful reform in the GFA and given dangers from volatile and poorly regulated capital flows, EMs have to continue with costly self-insurance. The low effect on India of the January taper reflected the success of the short-term measures the government and the RBI had taken, such as restricting gold imports. But longer-term measures continued to be necessary.

Although IMF funds are now inadequate to deal with potential outflows, Fed swaps are available only to a few, largely G-7 countries, with strong mutual interests. Participation in regional initiatives can help achieve a better balance of power and lead to more symmetric adjustment. Then, the financial reforms necessary to reduce leverage and strengthen the GFA may be implemented, and EMs gain more freedom to follow context-specific macroeconomic policies.

Table 2.8 Trends in money

	Reserve money	Narrow money	Broad money	Demand deposits	Time deposits
Average annual growth rate					
1950–1951 to 1959–1960	4.11	3.56	5.95	3.22	15.62
1960–1961 to 1969–1970	7.61	9.19	9.57	12.63	10.61
1970–1971 to 1979–1980	14.49	12.18	17.28	13.55	24.71
1980–1981 to 1989–1990	16.84	15.1	17.22	15.83	18.6
1990–1991 to 1999–2000	13.87	15.63	17.18	16.32	17.99
2000–2001 to 2009–2010	15.43	15.99	17.47	17.49	18.12
2010–2011 to 2012–2013	9.65	8.38	14.38	1.37	16.41
Average Ratio to GDPmp					
1951–1952 to 1959–1960	13.2	17.48	22.03	5.12	4.55
1960–1961 to 1969–1970	11.46	15.76	21.85	4.98	6.09
1970–1971 to 1979–1980	10.99	16.2	29.24	7.02	13.04
1980–1981 to 1989–1990	13.84	15.74	41.99	6.58	26.24
1990–1991 to 1999–2000	15.28	17.48	51.33	7.71	33.86
2000–2001 to 2009–2010	15.94	20.81	73.51	9.64	52.7
2010–2011 to 2012–2013	16.17	19.69	82.73	8.19	63.04

2.6 Trends in Money and Credit

The trends in money and credit[23] over the decades also demonstrate the policy issues surveyed. Table 2.8 shows much more fluctuations in the rate of growth of RM compared to other types of money. Rates of growth for all types increased substantially after the first two decades, demonstrating the increasing monetization of the economy. This was especially rapid from the 1980s as the jump in time deposit to GDP ratio, and of broad money, of which it is a component, indicates. The jump in time deposit ratios reflects the rise in savings ratios in the 1980s to above 20 % (Table 1.4). The expansion in bank branches partly caused this rise. In the post-GFC period, broad money compensated somewhat for a slower growth of reserve money, showing the limits to control of monetary aggregates in a more developed financial system.

[23] RBI definitions of reserve money from the components side are: Currency in circulation + Banker's deposits with the RBI + other deposits with the RBI, and from the sources side: RBI's domestic credit + Government's currency liabilities to the Public + Net FX assets of RBI other items. The definitions of broad money from the components side are: Currency with the public + Aggregate deposits with banks, and from the sources side are: Net bank credit to government (Net RBI credit to central and state governments + other banks' credit to government) + Bank credit to commercial sector (RBI + other banks) + Net forex assets of banking sector (RBI + other banks) + Government's currency liabilities to the public—banking sector's net non-monetary liabilities. These were followed in deriving the series given in the tables.

Table 2.9 Decadal averages

	D/R	D/C	Money multiplier	M3/RM	GDP/M3
1953–1954 to 1959–1960	21.61	0.79	1.73	1.69	4.7
1960–1961 to 1969–1970	28.09	1.09	2.01	1.93	4.83
1970–1971 to 1979–1980	19.5	2.12	2.72	2.66	3.77
1980–1981 to 1989–1990	8.07	3.45	3.09	3.12	2.58
1990–1991 to 1999–2000	8.29	4.18	3.43	3.37	2.11
2000–2001 to 2009–2010	14.8	5.42	4.67	4.73	1.46
2010–2011 to 2012–2013	17.85	5.97	5.18	5.14	1.29

Table 2.9 presents select monetary ratios: the money multiplier and its determinants; the aggregate deposits-to-bank reserves ratio (D/R); and aggregate deposits-to-currency ratio (D/C). Currency and reserves are the quantity variables that can be affected by the CB. For example, the CB can increase currency by printing more money, although currency held does depend on the demand for it. It can also increase reserves by requiring a higher percentage of deposits to be stored in the CB.

The steady rise in D/C reflects monetization of the economy. It demonstrates confidence in the financial system, and the absence of inflation high enough to induce a flight from money. The fall in D/R from the 1970s was a consequence of the sharp rise in CRR. This was unable to prevent a rise in M/RM, but it did slow down its increase in the 1980s and 1990s compared to the last decade. The last column GDP/M is a measure of velocity. The latter fell through all the decades, showing a well-managed financial expansion, and a positive income elasticity of money demand.[24] Income elasticity was rising because of expansion of bank branches, but lack of other financial instruments probably tended to decrease it. GDP/M did rise for a few years in the inflationary 1970s, as did the GDP/C ratio. The GDP of the nation rose as it became a trillion dollar plus economy. But the stock of money, essential for lubricating commerce, rose even faster. The money multiplier continued to grow in the post-GFC period despite some rise in currency held because of higher inflation.

Table 2.10 shows the creation of credit, on which monetary policy was explicitly focused for much of the period. The steepest rise in credit/GDP ratios came, however, after liberalization. India's credit/GDP ratio is low by world standards and must rise. But a sudden sharp rise often leads to a financial crisis. Rates of growth of credit were, however, always moderate. Also noteworthy, in Table 2.10, is the sharp fall in RBI's credit to the government, following the termination of

[24] In the US, for example, velocity fell until 1948, the period of expansion of banks, and rose after that.

Table 2.10 Trends in credit

	Net RBI credit to central government	Net RBI credit to state government	Net RBI credit to government	Other bank investment in government securities	Net bank credit to government	RBI credit to commercial sector	Other bank's credit to commercial sector	Total bank credit to commercial sector	Total bank credit
Average annual growth rate									
1960–1961 to 1969–1970	-	-	7.12	8.9	7.5	30.42	16.15	15.45	10.94
1970–1971 to 1979–1980	14.19	27.02	13.93	20.34	15.58	38.47	18.7	19.13	17.54
1980–1981 to 1989–1990	19.9	29.47	19.69	19.18	19.41	15.81	17.31	17.21	18.09
1990–1991 to 1999–2000	7.12	18.41	7.49	21.15	14.22	10.63	14.76	14.56	14.37
2000–2001 to 2009–2010	−580.8	0.42	−510.58	17.71	14.81	42.75	19.98	19.68	17.56
2010–2011 to 2012–2013	44.12	18,381.03	44.25	13.34	17.57	41.06	17.53	17.54	17.55
Average Ratio to GDPmp									
1960–1961 to 1969–1970	-	-	10.02	3.02	13.04	0.14	9.55	9.69	22.74
1970–1971 to 1979–1980	8.39	0.66	8.96	4.51	13.57	0.81	17.77	18.57	32.14
1980–1981 to 1989–1990	12.79	0.55	13.34	7.3	20.65	1.14	27.26	28.39	49.05
1990–1991 to 1999–2000	10.6	0.28	10.88	11.77	22.65	0.75	27.98	28.73	51.39
2000–2001 to 2009–2010	2.08	0.17	2.24	21.32	23.5	0.15	43.45	43.6	67.17
2010–2011 to 2012–2013	5.63	0.02	5.65	20.65	26.30	0.03	55.34	55.38	81.67

Note Net RBI credit to state governments was INR 181 in 2008–2009 and INR 4.55 crore in 2009–2010

ad hoc treasury bills, and the imperatives of sterilization of large inflows. Other bank credit to the government rose. Banks often voluntarily held Gsecs in excess of lowered SLR requirements, as rates and returns became attractive. As capital inflows slowed, post-GFC RBI credit to the government rose since it could no longer meet its required balance sheet expansion through accumulation of foreign exchange reserves. As a result, other banks lent more to the commercial sector.

Although the size of the retail Gsecs market had seen a large rise, the fear of adversely affecting rates and increasing the cost of government borrowing restrained the RBI's use of OMOs. Complicated restraints on Gsecs and split between capital and interest with mark to market only for the part not held to maturity continued to make Gsecs attractive to banks and to prevent them from selling when they could make capital gains. The need for such restraints will reduce as a smaller share of held to maturity category and more interest rate volatility forces banks to hedge interest rate risks. Apart from OTC derivatives, there were also attempts to develop markets for interest rate futures.

Creating retail depth in the holding of Gsecs, and reducing the relative size of government borrowing from the domestic financial sector, will help the RBI to move more fully toward interest rate rather than money supply or credit variables as instruments. A push for change will come from the new Basel III prudential norms, which are unlikely to accept a forced statutory holding of even A class securities as providing a liquidity buffer. The new IFRS accounting norms will also require marking holdings of Gsecs to market.

In AEs, as debt shares declined, independent debt management offices were created. It was thought separating monetary policy from the management of the Government debt would reduce conflicts of interest. India was set to also follow this reform path. But as post-crisis debt levels in these countries rose sharply, CB market tactics became important in maintaining the confidence of market participants and smooth functioning of debt markets (Goodhart 2010). Given the relatively high levels of Government debt, the RBI had long been using such tactics to manage government borrowing requirements. Other countries seem to be converging to India's current practices even as India tries to converge to earlier norms. This underlines again that market development cannot mean blindly aping practices elsewhere. Adapting to local needs and structure is important.

Table 2.11 shows the rising share of Gsecs in the commercial banks portfolio and the consequent fall in share of commercial credit. The contribution of net domestic assets (NDA) to RM became negative as largenet foreign assets (NFA) displaced them in the RBI's balance sheet. Additions to foreign exchange reserves, driven by capital flows, exceeded the current account by a large margin. All these effects moderated in the post-GFC period as capital inflows reduced. Since reserves responded to volatile inflows on the capital account, while the current account was in deficit, they were a valid precautionary measure.

Table 2.11 Effects of reserve accumulation

Decades	Ratio of Net domestic assets to reserve money (RM)	Ratio of net foreign assets of the RBI to RM	Share of G securities in other bank credit	Share of commercial credit in other bank credit	Change in forex reserves as a ratio of current account of BOP (+, increase)
	%	%			
1960–1961 to 1969–1970	-	5.45	24.17	75.83	0.098
1970–1971 to 1979–1980	80.35	19.65	20.13	79.87	0.641
1980–1981 to 1989–1990	89.33	12.66	21.04	78.96	−0.069
1990–1991 to 1999–2000	62.13	37.87	29.5	70.5	1.69
2000–2001 to 2009–2010	−9.67	108.56	33.37	66.63	1.42
2010–2011 to 2012–2013	−0.95	100.85	27.17	72.83	0.36

2.7 Conclusion

Money and monetary policy are slippery concepts, and reality is often not what it seems on a surface reading. But careful fact-based analysis, using an appropriate analytical framework, yields interesting insights. There is two-way causality between money and nominal income. But during large supply shocks, policy shocks can be treated as exogenous. Such shocks are used in this study to understand the structure of the economy. The results validate the framework used. These suggest that policy was sometimes exceedingly tight when the fear and the common understanding were opposite: of a large monetary overhang. In focusing on financing the Government, rather than on domestic cycles, policy was procyclical—too accommodative in good times and tight in bad times.

Fiscal dominance pushed monetary policy to be too tight or too loose to compensate. An intellectual climate that encouraged government intervention and advocated a big push for development favored the dominance of fiscal policy. These ideas became embedded in institutions and created path dependence—it was difficult to break out on a new path. The balance of payments crisis and the change in intellectual ideas provided the opportunity. The initial swing was too much in favor of markets, but a series of international currency and financial crisis have helped to moderate orthodoxy. It has become possible to devise a middling through path that suits Indian democracy and structure. The global crisis evoked a refreshing and apt policy stance that helped the economy retain high growth. But the stimulus was continued too long and, together with multiple supply shocks, made inflation persistent. Improvements are still required in inflation management.

When the dominant ideas of the time supported closed capital-intensive import-substitutinggrowth, Vakil and Brahmananda (1956) pointed out the importance of the wage goods constraint. Relieving the latter required more attention on increasing agricultural productivity and on openness. But the closing of the economy that condemned India to many years of stagnation happened because intellectual opinion was too susceptible to external ideas and neglected more robust ideas based on a close understanding of own context.

The currently dominant ideas, favoring gradual liberalization, should aid India in its catchup period of high growth and beyond, providing high-productivity employment for its billion plus people. But that tailoring to context continues to be required. A non-ideological middling through approach makes a pragmatic adaptation to context possible. For monetary policy, the three factors that cause a loss of autonomy—governments, markets, and openness—are conveniently moderating each other. Thus, markets are moderating fiscal profligacy; crises are moderating markets and openness. And institutions are slowly strengthening in adapting to the new ideas.[25]

The many changes recorded in this history demonstrate the dynamism displayed by the economy, its institutions, and policy, countering the argument that

[25] A threatened downgrade by credit rating agencies forced a reduction in the fiscal deficit in 2013.

democracies are doomed to stagnation. An example of change is the behavior of interest rates. Although liberalization initially increased the volatility of rates in a thin market, it eventually brought down the volatility to levels prevailing when rates were tightly administered, as markets deepened. But now, the rates came through a robust interaction between markets, institutions, and policy.

In the mid-1990s, in thin markets and with greater monetary autonomy combined with unhealthy government finances, there were sharp peaks in policy and market rates that hurt growth. But immediately after the GFC, when fiscal responsibility legislation, higher growth, and better tax administration had improved government finances, monetary–fiscal coordination improved and India came through in better shape. In hindsight, the post-GFC stimulus was too large and continued too long, while exchange rates were left too much to volatile capital flows, although alternative polices were available. So learning must continue. But even so, the future will see these years as transformative for India and its institutions. Sometimes, the best haste is made slowly.

References

Agarwal A (2008) Inflation targeting in India: an explorative analysis, Chap 2. Unpublished IGIDR PhD thesis

Christiano LJ, Eichenbaum M, Evans CL (1999) Monetary policy shocks: what have we learned and to what end? Handbook of Macroeconomics, Chap 2, 1:65–148

Curdia V and Woodford M (2010) Conventional and unconventional monetary policy. Federal Reserve Bank of St. Louis Review 92(4): 229–264. July/August

Dash S, Goyal A (2000) The money supply process in India: identification, analysis and estimation. Indian Econ J 48(1). July–September

GFI (Global Financial Integrity) (2010) Drivers and dynamics of illicit financial flows from India: 1948–2008. http://india.gfip.org. Accessed Sept 2011

Goodhart C (2010) The changing role of central banks. BIS Working Papers no 326. www.bis.org/list/wpapers/index.htm. Accessed 2011

Goyal A (1999) The political economy of the revenue deficit. In: Parikh KS (ed) India development report. IGIDR and Oxford University Press, New Delhi

Goyal A (2005) Reducing endogenous amplification of shocks from capital flows in developing countries. GDN project report. http://www.gdnet.org/pdf2/gdn_library/global_research_projects/macro_low_income/Goyal.pdf. Accessed 2010

Goyal A (2008) Macroeconomic policy and the exchange rate: working together? In: Radhakrishna R (ed) India Development Report 2008, Chap 7. IGIDR and Oxford University Press, New Delhi, pp 96–111

Goyal A (2009) Financial crises: reducing pro-cyclicality. Macroecon Finan Emerg Market Economies 2(2):173–183

Goyal A (2011a) A general equilibrium open economy model for emerging markets: monetary policy with a dualistic labor market. Econ Model 28(2):1392–1404

Goyal A (2011b) Exchange rate regimes and macroeconomic performance in South Asia. In: Jha R (ed) Routledge Handbook on South Asian Economies

Goyal A (2012a) India's fiscal and monetary framework: growth in an opening economy. Macroeconomics and finance in emerging market economies, Chap 12, 5(1). In: Goyal A (ed) Macroeconomics and markets in India. Routledge, UK. Earlier version available at http://www.igidr.ac.in/pdf/publication/WP-2010-025.pdf

Goyal A (2012b) Propagation mechanisms in inflation: governance as key. In: Mahendra Dev S (ed) India development report 2012, Chap 3. IGIDR and Oxford University Press, New Delhi, pp 32–46

Goyal A (2014a) External shocks. In: Mahendra Dev S (ed) India development report 2014. IGIDR and Oxford University Press, New Delhi

Goyal A (2014b) Banks, policy, and risks: how emerging markets differ. Int J Public Policy 10(1, 2, 3):4–26

Goyal A and Arora S (2013) Inferring India's potential growth and policy stance. J Quant Econ 11(1 & 2):63–80. January–July

IMF (International Monetary Fund) (2013) Global impact and challenges of unconventional monetary policies. IMF Policy Paper. October

IMF (International Monetary Fund) (2014) How do changes in the investor base and financial deepening affect emerging market economies? In: Global financial stability report: Moving from liquidity- to growth-driven markets, Chap 2. http://www.imf.org/External/Pubs/FT/GFSR/2014/01/pdf/c2.pdf. Accessed 4 Apr 2014

Jalan B (2001) Monetary and credit policy for the year 2001–2002. Statement by Dr. Bimal Jalan, Governor, Reserve Bank of India. www.cpolicy.rbi.in. Accessed Apr 2010

Mohanty D (2010) Perspectives on inflation in India. Speech given at the Bankers Club, Chennai, 28 Sept

Ostry J, Ghosh A, Korinek A (2012) Multilateral aspects of managing the IMF Staff Discussion Note. 7 Sept

Rangarajan C (2002) Indian economy: essays on money and finance. UBS Publishers, New Delhi

Rangarajan C (2004) Select essays on Indian economy, vol 1, 2. Academic Foundation, New Delhi

RBI (Reserve Bank of India) (1985) Report of the committee to review the working of the monetary system. (S. Chakravarty, Chairman), Bombay

RBI (Reserve Bank of India) (2011) Report of the working group on operating procedures of monetary policy (Chairman: D. Mohanty)

RBI (Reserve Bank of India) 2014 India's International Investment Position (IIP), Quarter ended December 2013. http://rbi.org.in/Scripts/BS_PressReleaseDisplay.aspx?prid=30899

Reddy YV (2002) Lectures on economic and financial sector reforms in India. Oxford University Press, New Delhi

Thomson A (2012) G20 eases push for deficit cutting. Financial Times. November. Accessed Jan 2013 from http://www.ft.com/intl/cms/s/0/c68ff436-279b-11e2-abcb-00144feabdc0.html#ixzz2NE3OIMeL

Thorat U (2010) Learning from crises. Macroecon Finan Emerg Market Economies 3(2):299–307

Vakil CN, Brahmananda PR (1956) Planning for an expanding economy: accumulation employment and technical progress in underdeveloped countries. Vora and Co, Bombay

Index

A. Goyal, *History of Monetary Policy in India Since Independence*,
SpringerBriefs in Economics, DOI 10.1007/978-81-322-1961-3

FSC
www.fsc.org

MIX
Papier aus verantwortungsvollen Quellen
Paper from responsible sources
FSC® C105338

If you have any concerns about our products,
you can contact us on
ProductSafety@springernature.com

In case Publisher is established outside the EU,
the EU authorized representative is:
Springer Nature Customer Service Center GmbH
Europaplatz 3, 69115 Heidelberg, Germany

Printed by Libri Plureos GmbH
in Hamburg, Germany